THE DOOR-TO-DOOR SALES POCKET BIBLE

How to make **a ton of money** selling door-to-door without lying, cheating, or pissing (many) people off.

Kim Robinson

authorHOUSE®

AuthorHouse™
1663 Liberty Drive
Bloomington, IN 47403
www.authorhouse.com
Phone: 833-262-8899

Published by AuthorHouse 06/21/2021

ISBN: 978-1-6655-2916-7 (sc)
ISBN: 978-1-6655-2915-0 (e)

Library of Congress Control Number: 2021912499

Print information available on the last page.

Contents

Chapter 6: Overcoming Objections............. 101
When does the act of selling begin?

Introduction

Why you want to read this book

You were a weird kid if you dreamed of becoming a commission-only door-to-door sales rep when you grew up.

I did not think I was a weird kid, and I certainly never dreamed of becoming a commission-only door-to-door salesman when I grew up, but sometimes shit happens, and you have to do what you have to do to survive. Well, shit happened to me when I was in my mid-30s, and I became a commission-only, door-to-door salesman. I went on to make a career of it and made a ton of money in the process. So who knows, maybe I was a weird kid after all...

Whether or not you were a weird kid dreaming of a career in door-to-door sales, someone looking for something different, or are a current rep seeking a much higher income, this book will show you in a clear, step-by-step process how to become and remain a consistent sales-generating professional without having to lie to prospects, cheat, and steal from your company or piss (many) people off. It is truly a step-by-step, how-to

Bible for anyone and everyone who wants to make money selling products and services door-to-door.

I fell into the job after earning a college degree and enjoying good financial success for a number of years. I was living large and life was good—right up until it wasn't. A couple of poor choices here, a couple of bad calls there, and...Ka-Boom! My business collapsed, and I had to file Chapter 11 bankruptcy. I was flat broke and in such desperate need of a job that I answered an ad by the local cable TV company looking for door-to-door sales reps solely because it offered two weeks of paid training to new hires. Did I want to be a door-to-door salesman? Absolutely not. But two weeks' guaranteed pay? I was in.

My arrogance was such that I had no intention of actually becoming a door-to-door sales rep. I, as many people did then and still do today, saw door-to-door sales as a job filled mostly by people who dropped out of high school and were just a step away from being homeless. I was an educated man! I still had a nice apartment. I wasn't like those "other guys." I just needed a few bucks to tide me over until a "real" job came along, and two weeks of paid training would put at least some money in my pocket while I looked for something else, so I took the job.

Nothing better came along during my two weeks of paid training, so I decided to at least go knock on a few doors and see if I could stumble into a few sales to pick up a few more bucks. And "stumble" was exactly what I did; as I went out to sell, it was immediately clear that I was unprepared for the job because my training failed to adequately cover important stuff like *what do I say when they open the door?*

With no more training pay coming in and zero effective tools for the job, I went out with what I did have: a clipboard, some order forms, a smile on my face, and a willingness to speak with anybody. I figured my chance of actual success to be somewhere between zero and never, but why not give it a shot? Maybe I would get lucky enough to pick up a few extra bucks while I searched for a "real" job.

Much to my surprise, I made two big sales in just a couple of hours on my first night, and the commission money I earned in that short period of time was more than a full day of the training pay, so I thought I'd hang around a few days more. The next night I made another two sales. And two more the night after that. After earning more money in commissions from just three evenings of knocking on doors than I did attending the training class full-time for two weeks, I made one of the smartest decisions of my life—I quit looking for something better and gave this job my full attention.

I was just making it up as I went along, but I wasn't a total novice to sales. I had worked in sales off and on for most of my life, and I was already familiar with the consultative sales process. This meant that once I was able to get the person who opened the door to engage with me and have a sales conversation, I could more often than not make the sale. The hard part was getting people, who didn't know I existed until they opened their door and saw my smiling face on their porch, to speak with me. I tried everything imaginable at the door to get the prospect to engage. I pretended to be an auditor, *We had a service issue recently, and I am out auditing customer service. Oh, you don't have our service? Well, I must have the address wrong, but I can offer you a...* and so it went. I made sales basically by telling lies to start the conversation and then moving on from there. My production was terribly inconsistent, and my soul was taking a (small) hit by my inventive dishonesty. But I was making sales and earning commissions, so I knew that I could make more money if I would quit winging it and nail down a set process that would help me consistently start more conversations with prospects at the door.

So, I did. I figured out how to consistently start the sales conversation without lying to the prospect about who or what I was.

Through the trial-and-error process of knocking on doors and applying some of what I learned by earning a degree in behavioral psychology, I created a unique process that enabled me to consistently start a sales conversation at the door with someone who didn't know I existed until they met me on their porch. I applied that same process at every door, regardless if it opened into a mansion or a rusted-out Airstream trailer on blocks. My opening process consistently got me past the door, into the dwelling and the actual sales conversation about my products and services. My sales and income took off like a rocket. Turns out that selling door-to-door was a real job after all.

Back in the early '90s, I made enough money as a commission-only salesman selling cable TV subscriptions in heavily remarketed areas to buy a home near the coast just south of San Francisco. And in using my unique opening to make those sales, I never lied to prospects, cheated the company (recycling bad debt customers by using a fake name to reconnect service was a common practice among my peers at the time), or risked injury by putting my foot in the door to keep the prospect from closing it.

In 2005, I figured I was about as expert at door-to-door sales as anyone could be, so I launched my own sales training company to teach people how to sell their stuff door-to-door. In 2008 I began putting my classes, courses, and sales tips on video, and to date, thousands of direct sales reps all over North America, Mexico, the Americas, and parts of Europe have attended my workshops or watched my step-by-step sales training videos to learn how to become and remain successful door-to-door sales representatives for their cable TV companies, and within the last few years, pest control salespeople as well. Since transitioning into being a full-time sales trainer, my personal and professional goal has been to arm people who want to make money at sales (whether they dreamed of the career as a weird kid or not) with the tools they need to succeed. Simple as that.

I believe that door-to-door sales, when done right, is not a whole lot more than walking down the street talking to people. There are tough parts about it, of course; your company is not looking to pay a whole bunch of money to people for something that's unbelievably easy, but it is nowhere near as hard as poorly trained people who struggle at it make it out to be. Nor as difficult as I thought it was when I first stumbled around in the field after my two weeks of "training." I earned a lot of money in commission-only, door-to-door sales, and I always tried to have fun while doing it. You can, too.

In this book, I will show you how to become and remain a successful door-to-door salesperson. Period. It is a quick read but with a great deal of content, so please read the book straight through from start to finish and then use it as a direct reference guide to help you master every step of the process from approaching a door to walking away with a closed sale. It is your book, so mark it up! Highlight the critical passages and make it a habit to go back and review everything and use the blank pages at the end of the book to write notes.

I agree with the popular sentiment that 90% of success is just showing up, but that only applies if you spend the other 10% learning your craft—whatever it is. An auto mechanic needs to learn about cars before s/he "just shows up," and the same law applies to sales and selling. You bought my book, so you are on the path to fully embrace that critical 10%.

The book is broken down into an effective step-by-step informational process, beginning with specific fundamental mechanics of the job and a basic understanding of what it takes to become, and remain, a successful salesperson. Picking up a few bucks here and there is fine when you're winging it, but the fact-based content and proven lessons I spell out in this book will help you consistently make more sales door-to-door and earn more money. Since the essence of sales and selling is communication, the contents of this book will also help you more clearly and effectively communicate with others in both business and personal relationships for the rest of your life. Become more successful and communicate better...what's not to like about that?

Good luck and good selling!

The Mechanics of the Job

Important stuff I wish to hell
I knew when I started

Competition for telecommunications services and pest control companies is everywhere and getting tougher every year. If you don't feel that you can offer customers a good value selling the product(s) or services of the company you represent, then do yourself a favor and go to the competitor that can offer a better service and value. Selling is easier if you believe in what you sell—especially in a competitive environment—which also helps avoid lying, cheating, or pissing (many) people off.

But if you are confident in your employer, then pay attention to this news bulletin: the competitive products and services that are similar to those you sell are also good quality. Maybe not as good (see above) but in today's hot, competitive marketplace, unless you are selling telephone service against a competitor offering two cans connected by a string, then the services provided by your competitors are going to be on a par with those you offer. Period. Never denigrate the competition in hopes of making your stuff look better in comparison because their stuff is not crap, and you insult the intelligence of everyone who purchased from the "other guy." Remember—insult a product and you insult the person who bought it, and an insult is not a good way to start or maintain a sales conversation.

You will run into people who tell you they are happy with what they have and therefore see no reason to switch to your company. What they already have is good. They're used to it, so they see no reason to switch. It is for these people that you are reading this book. Because in a competitive environment, you have to be able to comfortably and conversationally guide customers of your competitor into seeing **all on their own** that what they really want to have is what you sell. You can do this, and you can do it without putting down the competition.

It is a fact that success in this position is not tied to previous sales experience. I have seen many, many people with no sales experience at all find terrific success in this job because they came into it with an open mind, with a strong work ethic, and readily eager to learn.

Of course, some or even a lot of previous sales experience may help, and it certainly doesn't hurt, but when I came into this job with previous sales experience, I quickly learned (like on Day #1) that there is a world of difference between prospects coming to you in a traditional retail environment, and you going to them where they do not know you're coming. Truly, a world of difference that retail workers assessing the difficulty of door-to-door sales definitely underestimate. When I started, I needed to check my veteran salesman ego at the door and teach myself the fundamental mechanics of field sales as I went along, starting with how to begin the conversation with a prospect who doesn't know I exist until they open their door and meet me on their porch. I learned very quickly that my extensive sales experience, knowledge of the consultative sales process, and veteran salesman ego didn't mean a thing until after the conversation began. You can't close a sale you can't open.

Another mistaken assumption about door-to-door salespeople is that we are all pushy, obnoxious types who shove our feet into doors to keep them open, while we verbally vomit onto the prospect everything possible about our products and prices. That is certainly true about a lot of reps, but those who act like that don't do very well or last very long.

Telecommunication and pest control services are highly competitive and remember that your competitor has good products, so aggressive badgering people at the door will kill any hope of earning a consistent, high level income.

Consistent high-level success is based 100% on comfortable and sincere communication between you and the prospect.

Consultative door-to-door sales is both a discipline and a process. And the mechanics are such that if you show the discipline to follow the proven process of time and territory management, using a professional Opening At The Door, and use the steps of the consultative sales process once the conversation is started, then you will be successful. Looks and gender don't mean a thing if you follow the mechanics.

Please keep in mind that hearing NO is part and parcel of being a salesperson. If your prospect does not say no at any time during your presentation then you are a customer service agent simply helping that customer get what they already know they want. Great! Sadly that does not happen very often in door-to-door sales. Nos come early and often in this profession and those salespeople who give up after they hear just one or even two, are leaving money on the table that could be in their pocket. As salespeople, our job is to turn nos into yeses.

Additionally, door-to-door sales is **not** just a numbers game where every **no** you hear brings you closer to a **yes**. That philosophy is just plain BS and was created by people who do not know how to sell, so they just look for people who already want to buy what they sell. With this job, it is hard enough just to catch people at home, so when you do and they say **no** to your opening, you don't just walk away but follow a process to overcome their no to get the sale off on the right foot.

Take a surgeon for example. If something goes wrong in surgery and some kind of a **no** appears that prevents completing the operation as planned, a highly trained professional surgeon does not give up and say... "Oh well. Better luck with the next patient." Of course not! The surgeon does not panic or give up the ship but instead, follows the process s/he learned to handle it confidently. This is an educated discipline. If you are **not ready** for the "what if," or **no** in sales, then you are wasting a lot of time and energy and leaving a lot of money on the table by not getting past that no to make a sale.

Unlike surgeons (thank goodness), a disciplined sales pro expects to hear **no**, I certainly don't want to be operated on by a surgeon who expects something to go wrong. EGADS! But in sales, getting a **no** is part and parcel of the job, and that's where discipline comes into play. The stakes in surgery and sales are obviously very different, but the importance of resilience informed by training is true of both. When you hear **no**, you do not fall off your game and think, "oh well, better luck at the next door," you remember your training, respond appropriately, and move on. It is part of the sales process and what makes for success.

Overcoming an objection—a **no**—in a comfortable and conversational manner is the mark of a true sales professional adhering to the consultative sales process. As long as there is a conversation with both people talking and listening, it is consultative selling. Persistence is not badgering if there is a balanced conversation occurring.

It is pushy and obnoxious badgering when a sales rep is doing all of the talking or being confrontational.

This should come as no surprise, but the most important fact about direct sales is that the Opening At The Door (OATD), is everything. Absolutely everything. I have seen many people who fashion themselves experts at the consultative sales process fail miserably at this job because they simply could not start a cold-call sales conversation at the door. Period. And I have witnessed many instances of people with poor sales skills do very well selling door-to-door simply because they were good at starting conversations and getting past the door. Selling is a learned skill, and when people who **can** start cold-call sales conversations learn the sales process of how best to move forward **after** they start the conversation, they knock it out of the park with a steady high-level income.

Personality & Character

There are two absolute requirements for success in this job that come in addition to learning the sales process from start to finish, and they are **personality and character**. Failure is certain without them both. **Personality** means that you've got to be someone with whom people like to speak. In short, don't be a jerk. Hard-nosed, aggressive jerks are annoying and don't cut it very long in this job because who wants to willingly spend time with an annoying person?

This is cold-call sales, and people don't know you from Adam when they open their door, so simply being nice is critical. In this job, **nice people do finish first**. As for character, along with the incredible positive benefit of personal freedom in this job where you are not stuck in a cubicle but outside basically building and running your own business, you need to have the **character** to go out and work when you are supposed to work. The character to get off the couch (it's cold outside…), go out the door, and go to work. Character really does count.

I speak from personal experience when I say that the hardest door to pass through is often your own front door. Believe me, I get that. It takes character to pass through that door when you don't feel like it. It takes character to pass through that door when the weather stinks. It takes character when a friend tries to get you to "take the night off" and do something else. Regardless of the temptation, people of character get off the couch, go through that door, and go to work. Period.

I will show you in this book the step-by-step sales process to make sales, but the pleasant personality and strong character are totally up to you.

Focus on What Makes You Money

Great reps, the ones at the top of the commission plan who earn a great living, focus their actions on things that lead directly to making sales and earning commissions, and they spend as little time as possible on things that may be work-related, but don't necessarily lead directly to making sales!

I feel compelled to mention this because many times I meet new hires who think, "Well, I spent time in in the office and made some copies of stuff and then had a few nice chats with other reps and put in my 40 hours for the week so I'm good." Okay, you're at work, but is any of that activity putting money in your pocket? No, it isn't. What puts money in your pocket is making sales which only come from spending time in the field, knocking on doors, and making sufficient, valid contacts every day. No shortcuts here. Your earnings are directly related to being in the field. This is an outside sales job. Not a hang around the office job. So go outside!

You might be the very best on the team at delivering the OATD or overcoming objections, but if you are not in the field delivering them to prospects—who cares? Your earnings are directly related to making sales while in the field. Your job is to sell. Period. A very sharp sales manager I once had told me that she didn't mind a messy desk or the occasional late memo as long as I was turning in the sales.

Attitude

Attitude in sales is everything. Everyone has both good and bad things happen to them—it's called life. And when a good thing happens to a positive person, the good thing is acknowledged and recognized as an **expected event**. An "of course" moment. *I've been working very hard for that to happen, and it did. Of course.* The good thing was **expected to happen and it did, thereby becoming a self-fulfilling prophecy.** And when a bad thing happens to a positive person, which happens because bad things occasionally happen to everybody, the bad thing is acknowledged, *Bummer,* dealt with, and moved past. A positive person immediately then looks for the next good thing to happen–the next *of course* moment because that's what they *expect* to happen and are therefore working to achieve it.

When a good thing happens to a negative person, on the other hand, the good thing is not expected so it is met with suspicion. It is acknowledged with a *yeah, but* scenario. **Yeah,** *that was okay,* **but** *it won't happen again.* When a bad thing happens to a negative person, the bad thing is acknowledged and embraced as an expected occurrence. *I knew it. I just knew that deal wouldn't work out.* Their negative attitude means they expect things to fall apart and when they do, the bad thing becomes **a self-fulfilling prophecy**. *I knew it! It was too good to be true.* Or most common, *Just my luck!*

Someone's attitude is rarely so black and white. Few people with genuinely negative attitudes are even in sales. However, just like the power of the Dark Side portrayed in the Star Wars movies, it is easy for positive people to slip to the dark side and embrace a negative attitude if they are not vigilant at maintaining their positive outlook. Many times all it takes is a series of small missteps that can build-up to the point where they get in the way of being a pleasant person, which harms your sales success and gets in the way of realizing your dreams.

Attitude Tune-Up

Excitement and positive attitudes are contagious. People like being around people with positive attitudes because being positive is uplifting, and prospects will be more likely to have conversations with you and welcome you into their home if you are a person who projects positivity. When you knock on a door, **expect** them to want to speak with you so that when they do, it becomes a self-fulfilling prophecy, and when they don't, you're surprised, which makes it easier for you to be confident in your immediate attempt to overcome any objection they voice to get the sales conversation on track.

Here are a couple of tips to give yourself an attitude tune-up and prevent slipping to the Dark Side of negativity. First, **never ever say** *just my luck* when a bad thing happens to you. You have great luck! You live in the richest, most powerful nation on Earth, and you have a good job where you can earn enough money to realize your wildest dreams. That is a foundation of good luck.

Next, start your day off right with a positive affirmation. Every morning before you go out and meet the day, look yourself right in the eye in the mirror and give yourself a positive affirmation. Say, **out loud,** something **positive about yourself** in the present tense and repeat it five times. Say anything, as long as it is personal, positive, and present tense. I am as serious as a heart attack about the impact this simple daily act will have on both your attitude and your life. I have started my days this way for a very long time. Ever since I met the World's Greatest Salesman a long time ago...

I paid $20 when I was in my 20s (a lot to me at the time) to hear Joe Girard speak. He was a car salesman who was listed at the time in the Guinness Book of World Records as the World's Greatest Salesman because of his sales success. To wit: During the first gas crisis in the 1970s, gasoline shot up in a very short period of time from around $0.25 per gallon to well over a dollar. That amount seems super cheap to us now, but, at the time, it represented a rapid price increase of about 400%. Additionally, American auto manufacturers back then didn't pay a lot of attention to gas mileage and embraced the philosophy of simply installing bigger gas tanks to increase a car's driving radius. In a word, gas mileage sucked. Detroit built gas guzzlers, and Joe Girard was a salesman at a car lot that sold gas-guzzling General Motors cars. Even though car sales plummeted across the board due to the gas crisis, Joe Girard managed to **average over one new car sale a day** selling big gas guzzler GM cars. Not as a sales manager with others selling for him, and not small cars with better mileage, but as a single salesman selling big, high commission gas guzzlers! I read about him and figured that he was doing something right, so when I saw an ad for an upcoming in-person presentation, I dug deep and paid the twenty bucks for a ticket to hear him speak.

Joe was a terrific and very likable speaker and to my surprise, he did not speak about a specific sales process much at all but, instead, the importance of having a good attitude to succeed in sales and to living a good life. He recommended we all start the day with a positive affirmation, and he assured us that if we did that, our attitudes would improve and the world around us would look better. I took him at his word (after all, I paid $20 to hear him say it!), and practically every day since then I have looked myself in the eye and said something good about myself to myself. Really. I basically repeat what he urged us all in the audience to say, which is: *I am good. I am great. I am number one, and today is a great day.* I often add *good things happen to positive people. I am a positive person and good things happen to me.* If you do this and repeat a personal positive mantra every day for 30 days, I guarantee that your general attitude will improve, and you will see a positive change in the world around you. It really works.

Going bankrupt and having to start all over in my 30s was truly a crappy thing that happened to me. But I am a positive person, so I acknowledged the situation as the bad thing it was and then sought something positive out of it and became a very successful commission-only, door-to-door salesman.

I believe that if you start every day with a positive attitude tune-up and work hard to see the good in people and to make good things happen, they will.

Professional Behavior

Punctuality is a fundamental component of professionalism. Being punctual assures that you won't miss anything but also shows respect for every other person included in your interaction. Prospects appreciate punctual people because being punctual shows that you are reliable, organized, and serious about your job.

In the workplace, punctuality for meetings or work events shows your co-workers the same thing. Nobody should have to wait for you because you are so disrespectful or disorganized you can't be on time. It's rude, and if people are offended when you are late, they should be; it's disrespectful. Take sales meetings... coming in late and disturbing a meeting is an insult to everyone there. You might as well walk in and call every person there dumb, stupid, or lazy; it is an insult, and don't fool yourself into thinking others will assume you are important or busier than them because you are late. And by being there, it means being present—not on the phone, not checking your email, not texting—fully present and fully engaged, listening and participating. Being an adult.

If it's a video or teleconference call and you are typing or making noise or people or pets are making noise in the background, it is disruptive—which is not being present and prepared. Companies don't have meetings for fun, so be professional and show up on time and be prepared to listen and to participate.

Professional behavior in the house is how you conduct yourself in somebody's home. Regardless of whether it's a mansion or a rusted old Airstream, be respectful. Wipe your feet and ask if you should remove your shoes, etc. Be respectful to others to earn respect from them.

A critical component of professionalism is following through. Always complete your work, meet your commitments, and don't leave anything hanging. Do what you say you will do. Double-check appointment dates, leave-behinds, get back on unanswered questions—complete and thorough follow through on everything until the service you sold to a prospect is connected or delivered. Remember, it is how you get paid. Just finish.

Know Your Numbers

When I say, "know your numbers," I am not talking about birth dates or lottery picks. I am talking about the number of doors on which you knocked, contacts made, presentations delivered, sales entered, and sales completed. These are the numbers that help you manage your success. Professional sales reps who earn a great income can all recite their numbers any time they are asked! Without exception. Every time I meet a sales rep I ask, *What are your numbers?* And I can tell right away by their response how well they are doing. Top people making good money can recite their numbers accurately without hesitation. Those who hem and haw or simply shrug, I can tell are not cutting it and are most likely on their way out the door to another job.

By tracking approaches (doors knocked), contacts (someone opens the door) and presentations (they bite on your opening and you are into your sales conversation) and, of course, sales closed, you will be able to tell what parts of your individual sales process you need to improve so that both the quantity and quality of your sales rise. If approaches are high but contacts are low, then get out there when people are home (Saturday and Sunday). If contacts are good but presentations are low, then your OATD needs work (Chapter #2). And if your presentations are good but closed sales are low, then your sales skills need improvement (Chapters #3, #4, and #5).

On top of tracking your numbers for generating sales, also track your numbers regarding achieving your personal goals. Are you on track to buy a newer car? A nicer place to live? A college fund for your kids? Know what is important to you and write down the numbers you need to generate to achieve your goals. I'm talking about your life, so take charge of it and move forward.

Achieving your goals may come down to the extra effort of just a couple of extra contacts a day. If you know the numbers you need to achieve your goal and if you know exactly where you are at any given time relative to achieving that goal, then you will always know exactly what you need to do to achieve it. This is part of being professional. I believe in the saying, "Fail to plan and you will plan to fail," so identify your goals and know what you have to do every day to achieve them. My primary goal when I was a commission-only sales rep for the cable company in San Francisco was to buy a home in the suburbs and move my family out of our crowded apartment in the city. I created a plan to know how many sales I needed to make every week to achieve that goal, and I **religiously** followed that plan. (This is The Door-to-Door Sales Pocket **Bible** after all!) If I was short of my weekly sales and income goal on Friday, then I worked Saturday. If I was still short after working Saturday, then I worked on Sunday. I had a goal of owning my own home, and by accurately tracking all aspects of my sales activity, I was able to stay on track to achieve my goal.

Just three years after being flat broke and starting a new career as a commission-only, door-to-door sales representative, I moved my growing family into our own home in the suburbs on the coast just south of San Francisco. So what do you want to achieve?

Turf Management: The Proven Three-Pass Process

Direct sales is an important sales channel because all the TV and radio ads and direct mailer pieces in the world will not get someone to change their mind if they are already happy with what they've got when they see the ads and get the mailers. *Cable TV? I've got Satellite. Pest control? I don't see any bugs. I'm good.* These erstwhile-contented consumers stay where they're at until **you** come to their door and engage them in a sales conversation to guide them into seeing, all on their own, that what you offer is what they would prefer to have, so they buy what you sell and make the switch. That is consultative sales.

But to make these sales, you need contacts. You have to catch people at home to be able to make sales. Duh. I developed a method of turf management that has been tested extensively by sales teams I've led and sales reps I've coached, and it works. I call this process to boost contacts the Three-Pass System because it puts you on their doorstep at different times of day, which increases the likelihood of finding folks at home.

Please note that I am writing this book during the 2020/21 pandemic, and due to the virus, a great number of people who used to go to an office every day now work from home. All projections predict that most people who now work from home will continue to do so after the pandemic passes, which is very good news for door-to-door salespeople.

Four to eight in the evening is still considered Prime Selling Time because that is traditionally when most people are home. But in the coming post-pandemic work-at-home economy, you will find people home at different times throughout the day. It is now more important than ever to be in and to be seen during the day in the neighborhood(s) where you work.

Start every workday the night before and plot out the specific "doors of opportunity" on which you plan to knock. Then, not too early, but well before noon, go to work. This **first pass** is when you hang doors, make contacts, and presentations and sales where possible. Continue following your work plan for a couple of hours and take a brief afternoon break. After the break, make your **second pass** over the same territory, starting at the first door you knocked that morning and continue past your earlier stopping point until you get to the four o'clock start of Prime Selling Time. You will find more people home, and more importantly, you will find some people who did not open their door to you in the morning opening their door to you in the afternoon. It just happens. Take a brief afternoon break to gain refreshment and then launch into your Prime

Time **third pass** over the same territory, starting with the first door that wasn't answered and go on until eight in the evening.

Do not doddle as you work your territory but walk quickly between addresses and always—**always**—wear a smile on your face and wave to every car and pedestrian you see. Consistent success is all about contacts, and a person is much more likely to open their door to someone who smiled and waved at them as they drove by than to someone they saw slowly ambling down the street wearing a tired frown.

Your daily presence established by following this proven Three-Pass System will let everyone in the neighborhood know that you belong there, which will definitely help you quickly build your sales pipeline.

Best Neighborhoods to Work

When I started, we all wanted neighborhoods with a lot of movement, and those were generally low-income areas. Cable TV service was still a luxury item then, and Internet service was solely dial-up (Hello AOL). Cable TV installation was expensive so people who lived in those areas didn't just call the cable company to get service. When reps went through those neighborhoods where money was tight, an offer of a **free installation with HBO free for a month** (or some similar offer) had a nice impact. We avoided high-end areas like the plague because people in those neighborhoods were willing to pay the installation fee, so they generally just called the company and placed their order. Penetration was very high and opportunity quite low.

Today's marketplace is much different. Competition between service providers is extremely common so middle class to high-end areas are now the best to work for cable reps because everyone in those areas already has some form of everything you sell! Everyone there has Internet, some form of video, mobile, and even landline phones (I still have my landline.), and now even security systems. The good news is that in these competitive areas where **service penetration** is at 100%, market penetration (the people who have **your** company instead of your competitor) is only about 50%. Think about it. 50% high-end prospects? Fully half of the people there are prospects to whom you can sell your better quality, higher-value services. That's opportunity!

Best Days to Work

This is not now, nor ever was a nine-to-five Monday through Friday job. Those days and times mean you are stuck in a cubicle doing something boring and not outside walking around, enjoying the air, and meeting new people. (See? Make it fun!) My working hours were fairly flexible and primarily guided by my income goal. I needed a consistent high-level income, and I worked until I achieved that income goal every commission cycle. I did take Mondays off because few people are in a good mood on Monday, and I **always** worked Friday evening because people are generally in a good mood then. Common sense. Duh!

Tuesday evening through Friday evening were usually sufficient, but if I did not hit my sales goal by Friday evening, then I worked on Saturday, and I was at my first door by 9 a.m. I worked straight to 11:30 or 12 before I took a break. Sure, I occasionally woke people up at 9, and when that happened, I sincerely apologized and went to the next door. But I kept starting at 9 because I knew that just because the people at one address were still asleep (and not happy I woke them up), the people who lived next door were already up, had eaten breakfast, and were getting ready to go somewhere. So by coming by in the morning I caught them before they left and made the sale. If you work Saturday, and I hope you do, then knock on your first door at nine and keep going for three hours or so. Then stop knocking for a few hours and do what you do on Saturdays but come back in the late afternoon/evening for a couple more hours.

Saturday evenings are great because people are back from their Saturday daytime activity. They're home and have got Sunday to look forward to and are generally in a good mood. I cannot count the times I worked Saturday evening and people would meet me with an *oh yeah, hi…come in,* and I would be invited inside to a party. I entered and chatted with people being friendly, and I invariably made sales. I once made three sales and a new friend at a barbeque! Be open and friendly, and you will meet new people and make sales. And be sure to always make follow-up appointments in non-primetime hours if possible. (That was what I did on Mondays.)

I always used Sunday afternoons/evenings as catch-up time because it was, and remains, **the best time of the week for contacts**. Sure, you will occasionally piss people off because, well, it's Sunday, and some people feel strongly about anyone working on Sunday, but I am all about meeting people and making sales. So, if everyone is home Sunday afternoon/evening, and I am behind on my sales goal, then so what. I am out to make contacts because contacts lead to sales, and I need a few sales. End of story.

It is worth noting that many times I took Monday through Thursday off because I hit my weekly sales numbers and achieved my weekly sales and income goals just working Friday evening and my Saturday and Sunday hours. Many times.

Five Fundamentals of Professional Sales Communication

Selling is all about communication. A professional salesperson is someone who can comfortably establish a rapport with a prospect and then comfortably walk them through the sales process.

To that end, here are Five Fundamentals of Communication that will help you become and remain a successful salesperson.

Fundamental #1—Don't Be A Badger: In a good sales conversation, the prospect speaks 80% of the time, and the salesperson—you—speak only 20% of the time. This means that four times as many words should come out of the prospect's mouth than yours. This 80/20 rule is fundamental because the needs for what you sell come out of the prospect's mouth, not yours. You accomplish this conversational imbalance by asking open-ended questions that get the prospect to speak at length about what they have and what they need, and all you have to do to be successful is **shut up and listen** to what they say. Most people in sales don't listen well and just wait to talk while the prospect speaks. But if you actually **listen** to what the prospect says (and don't just wait to talk) as s/he responds to your open-ended questions, then the prospect will tell you what you need to know to make the sale.

The overwhelming majority of salespeople try to talk the prospect into buying what they sell instead of seeing if what you have is something the prospect may want to purchase. They do this by flipping the rule on its head with them doing 80% of the talking and essentially badgering the prospect. They badger them at the door by throwing out their **best deal** and telling them all about it and peppering them with multiple closed questions about their current services in a crude attempt to uncover buyer needs. I call these amateurs badgers because they yak, yak, yak to prospects to get inside the house, and they **continue to yak, yak, yak** with repetitive closed-ended questions whenever they do get inside the house to try to identify needs. *Do you have this? Do you have that? How much do you pay?* Yak, yak, yak. Badgering is annoying and annoyed prospects don't buy. Period. Salespeople everywhere have talked themselves out of more sales than they have ever talked themselves into by badgering.

Fundamental #2—Product Knowledge: It is essential to know what you are talking about. It sounds easy, but then why do we all encounter sales reps who don't? My wife and I went car shopping one day and while seated in a car on the lot that we were interested in, I asked the salesman a question about one of the car's features. I was seated behind the steering wheel and he was to my right on the passenger side. To answer my question he actually leaned to his left and put his head between me and the steering wheel to look for the answer on the instrument panel.

We left without buying a car from that knucklehead.

It's important to know everything possible about what you sell, and it is equally important to know what your competitors have so that you will know what you can offer that they can't. If you know everything possible about your products and services, and you know everything about the competitor's products and services, then you can use the positive differences to boost the value of what you sell to take customers away from your competitor(s) and put more money in your pocket.

Fundamental #3—Enthusiasm: This does not mean I expect you to be a cheerleader jumping around on a porch...*Yay, my stuff is GREAT!!!* No. It simply means that you truly believe that your products and services are good to own and offer customers a good value. The saying, **"If you believe it others will too"** is spot on. Enthusiasm is contagious. Believe it and others will too.

Fundamental #4—Humor: Have a sense of humor. Really. Be able to laugh at yourself. Be comfortable with self-deprecating humor. Especially at the door. If you blow the opening and come off sounding like a fast-talking used car salesman, then cop to it. Look the prospect in the eye and admit it. Say something like, *Hey, I am blowing it. I sound like a fast-talking used-car salesman. Sorry.* Believe me, if you are coming across that way then the prospect is just about to interrupt with a *No, thanks* and close the door in which case you're sunk. But a bit of humor with a self-deprecating remark just might keep the sale above water and moving forward. It has for me! There have been many times that I have violated all the rules I write about in this book—especially the one about talking too much! Hey, it happens. Nobody is perfect. But whenever I see the prospect's eyes fade off because I'm talking too much or talking nonsense, then I just stop talking and close my mouth. Even midsentence if that's when I see the eye fade. I just shut my mouth, pause a moment, smile, and make a self-deprecating remark. Usually something like, *Hey, sorry about that. I sound like a used car salesman, please forgive me.* Many times, that light touch of unexpected humor will cause the prospect to smile as well. If the door stays open, I add, *But I am not a car salesman, I am a district sales rep and media expert with your local cable company, and I have this great value on media services. Where's a good place for us to sit down?* Sometimes it works and the sales process gets back on track.

A friend of mine sells pest control services and whenever he sees a bug on the ground while speaking with a prospect or client, he steps on it and makes sure the other person sees him do it, then he says, *That one's for free.* I think that's funny and so do others. It works! Use humor as much as possible. People like people who make them smile and laugh. So have a sense of humor!

Fundamental #5—Honesty: Honesty is absolutely fundamental to success. Always be honest. Never lie or misrepresent to make a sale. It is not worth it. Lies will always come back to bite you. Your company wants you to be honest—it is a job requirement and a true fundamental to success. If your company does not want you to be honest, you're at the wrong company. You need to have integrity. Period.

The first step in projecting an honest appearance and demeanor to others is to **never use the word honest** in conversation. Never. For a professional salesperson, honesty is assumed. Your job as a sales pro is to help people get what they need or want, and that is an honest and honorable thing to do. If you sell cable TV services, then you have a complex product line and people often need help understanding it all. You are the expert and experts don't lie. **Same with pest control**. There are a lot of pests, and people need an expert to know how to get rid of them. So be an expert and never say, *to be honest*. Ever. Because when you do, you imply that you may not have been honest up to that point, and for a sales professional who is an expert at his/her job, honesty should never be in question. I know "to be honest" is a very common expression that causes few people to question your overall honesty when you say it. But **if only one person out of twenty** does take it as a poor reflection on you and you lose that sale, then that is one lost sale too many. You don't need to say it to get your point across, because what you really mean by that expression is *to be candid* or *to be blunt*. So say, *Well, Mr. Prospect...to be candid I...*or *to be blunt, I...*

Another crucial part of the honesty fundamental is that you must answer truthfully when people ask what you do. You are a sales professional, so be proud of it. When I get a call from a telemarketer or a direct salesman comes to my house, regardless of their opening line, I cut to the chase and ask, "What are you selling?" because I know they are selling something. The instant they start hemming and hawing and back-pedaling to diminish the fact that they want me to buy what they sell, then they are toast because I don't believe they are honest or that they will be honest in the sales process. I am not an idiot (contrary to what my Ex says about me…) and if the stranger at my door isn't wearing a uniform or holding a huge cardboard check made out to me from Publishers Clearing House, then I know s/he is selling something s/he wants me to buy. Duh. By not coming clean and telling me what they are selling, they come across as possibly dishonest and untrustworthy. Hence, they are toast.

Full disclosure, I did all of these things from which I am steering you away. I pretended to be a repairman, an auditor, and even an installer at the 'wrong address,' and yes, I did make sales. But many times I lost the sale (and a bit of my self-respect) the moment the prospect realized that I pretended to be someone else and that I was, in fact, "just a salesman" (their words). When I embraced the fact that I am a salesman when asked, I regained my self-respect while earning a lot more money. I even made admitting I am a salesman an important part of my Opening At The Door process (as you will soon see…). Being honest about being a salesman shatters the common negative stereotype people have of door-to-door salespeople.

Sidebar to #5: An important point to make about the role of honesty in sales is that being honest does not mean you need to shoot yourself in the foot in the sales process by volunteering negatives about your product(s). I have heard many sales reps kill good sales opportunities by volunteering common drawbacks to their services **in the spirit of being honest**. EGADS! All products and services have some kind of drawbacks to their ownership. For cable reps, it could be a lack of short installation time frames, and for pest people, it could be limited serviceability after dark in some areas. Whatever the drawbacks are, it is **not your job to volunteer these drawbacks**. If you are asked specifically about installation windows or serviceability times, then by-all-means answer truthfully, but being honest does not mean you should volunteer reasons for them to turn you away.

Additionally, I have seen countless reps shoot themselves in the foot by volunteering the most common drawback there is—price—as part of their opening at the door thinking that their "super low" price is a benefit that will help them start the conversation. Spoiler alert: if you're thinking of using this method...the prospect will not slap their hand to their forehead when they hear your dollar number and exclaim, *OMG—You can give me that price? I'LL TAKE IT!!* Nope. Not gonna happen. Price is a drawback to the sale because it points out to the prospect that they will have to pay their hard-earned cash to get what it is you sell. Which, in turn, makes you just another stranger trying to get into their wallet, and they will close the door.

As an example of how volunteering prices can ruin a sale by killing the prospect's desire to buy, imagine you take your sweetheart, the love of your life, out to dinner for a special occasion at the best restaurant in town. It is fancy and expensive. The evening is going to cost you $400, but you're cool with that. Just the two of you. You have the money, and you are going to have a grand time.

The restaurant is fine dining, which means that it is expensive and you have to order everything a la carte. You are seated and the waiter arrives at your table to take your orders. The waiter is friendly and engaging, but after every single thing you order, the waiter mentions the price of that item. The overall price for the meal will be the same at the end of the evening as if he did not mention any prices...you are still going to spend $400, but by mentioning the price every time you order something, the waiter reminds you that you're spending a lot of money which gets in the way of enjoying your night out. Money becomes a roadblock to having a good time. Pre-dinner cocktails: $10 each, appetizers $12.95 each, entrées $32.95 each, and a baked potato $8.95 each. Good grief. By the time dessert rolls around and the love of your life wants to order a slice of pie with a cup of coffee and the waiter says, that'll be $12, you're sitting there thinking *Oh man, do you really need that pie?* Even though the evening will not cost more than you anticipated, the waiter's constant reminder of how much everything costs has reminded you that you are spending a lot of money, and your desire to make the purchase diminishes.

The point is that if you lead with price in your opening, the majority of prospects will just hear a stranger asking for money, and even if they would have enjoyed your product, the reminder of price becomes a roadblock in the process and a big obstacle to making the sale.

Do not volunteer drawbacks in the name of honesty and do not lead with a price of anything at the door. Offer the prospect something to buy in your opening based on value, and not just 'getting your best deal,' because **when you sell on value, price becomes secondary.**

Below are a few more things to pay attention to because they are all components of sales communication between you and your prospect.

Body Language

Poor body language can be a real deal killer, and it starts with violating people's personal space. When you knock on a prospect's door, never lose sight of the fact that you are a stranger, and strangers can be scary. After you knock on the door, don't stand right in front of the door. Take a step or two back and give them space. Take a step down if possible.

Expert use of body language at the door draws people to open their door. When the prospect can see you after you knock because of a storm door or side windows, take a big step back, and continue to step back a little bit more as they approach to the point where you are far enough away from their door that the prospect will feel safe opening the door—generally six-to-ten feet. The backward step is non-threatening and tends to draw people forward to open their door. It works. Try it out.

It's also worth noting that I am writing this during a pandemic responsible for the deaths of hundreds of thousands of Americans and millions worldwide. So for your own safety and that of your prospects, wear a mask and step back six-to-ten feet from the door after you knock. Few people will open their door—or keep it open more than a second—if they see a stranger on their porch standing too close and not wearing a mask. On the other hand, a stranger showing respect by wearing a mask and stepping back from the door identifies that person as a professional concerned about others.

Proper body language also means to keep your hands in front of you, plainly visible holding your clipboard or tablet with your ID showing, and a smile on your face. Remember, your goal at this point is for them to open their door, and if you appear sneaky, suspicious, or scary (wear a mask!), the likelihood of them opening the door plummets, and you're done. No sale. Go to the next door.

Final Note of Chapter #1

It is important to note that people who do all of the negative things I've mentioned (and more) do make sales. Reps with poor openings who exhibit poor body language still generate sales because anything will work once in a while. But—and this is a huge BUT—if you follow the sales process I lay out in this book, you will still pick up all of the sales you would have made to the people who respond to badgers with poor openings and rude people with poor body language, but you will also **sell to the people who are turned off by such behavior**. Learn the skills. Practice the skills. Be a professional. Make a ton of money.

2

The Opening at the Door

What the hell do you say to get past the #@$% Door!

You can't close a sale you can't first open. Consistent, high-level success depends heavily upon your ability to get strangers who answer your knock to agree to have a conversation with you about your products and services. No conversation, no sale, no income.

I wanted a high-level income and quickly learned that by just being friendly and without any set sales process that I could make some pretty good sales numbers and income. But "pretty good" would not get me to my goal of buying a nice home in the suburbs. Being "friendly" is an **ingredient** of a sales process, it is not a process in and of itself. I needed to consistently generate sales, so I needed to create a process that would consistently help me get past doors and into a sales conversation with prospects.

My close ratio once I got past the front door and inside the house to have a sales conversation was well over 90%. Yes, I am a good salesman, and a 90% close ratio is very good, but I believe that with door-to-door sales, even a mediocre salesperson can have a close ratio close to 80% just by being polite and respectful once they get inside.

I mentioned on page #1 that few normal kids ever dream of becoming a door-to-door salesman when they grow up, but many people do sell door-to-door when they're kids. I, like many young boys and girls, actually had a commission-only door-to-door sales job when I was just eight years old. I sold tickets to a big annual event for the Boy Scouts, and the commissions were the prizes awarded commensurate with tickets sold. The more tickets sold, the nicer the prize/commission. Lots of tickets sold earned a swell prize. Only a few sold earned a crappy participant ribbon.

The event was the annual fundraiser for the Boy Scouts in my area and was called the Fun-O-Rama. The top prize that would go to the boy who sold the most tickets was a 10-speed bicycle. Prizes for 2nd and 3rd place were pretty swell and a hell of a lot better than 4th place and below, but no prize could compare with a 10-speed bike. Yeow!

Back when I was eight years old, a 10-speed was the Cadillac of Youthful Transportation and as such, was expensive and rare. The rich kid on the block (his dad was a plumber) had a skinny-tire 3-speed bike and all the rest of us had fat tire, one-speed clunkers. Top speed for us was however fast we could peddle with our one gear, and that was it. But a 10-speed bike had skinny tires, super cool curved handlebars, and ten gears that would easily enable the peddler to achieve escape velocity. I wanted that bike. I needed that bike. I saw myself riding that bike down the street gathering envious looks from everyone who saw see me whiz by. *There goes Kim, the fastest kid in town. Wow...*

The Fun-O-Rama was such a big event (at least to us 8-year-olds) that I actually thought selling tickets would be easy. I just needed to put in the effort to sell enough to win the bike. The contest ran for a full two weeks and every day after school and all day Saturday and Sunday I went out with my tickets. I knocked on doors, and at every door, I asked the person who answered, *Do you want to buy tickets to the Boy Scout Fun-O-Rama?* The effort was there, but sadly, after eleven days of dedicated door knocking and with only three more days left in the fourteen-day contest, the number of people who said yes to me and bought a ticket was barely high enough to win a crappy ribbon.

I was toast. That 10-speed was peddling away from me at escape velocity.

Back then, my dad sold cars at night to support my sister, my mom, and me while he attended college during the day to become a teacher. He was doing pretty good at the car lot and on his rare night off, which coincided with my 11th day of crappy ticket sales, he asked me how my sales were going. I told him not good because nobody wanted to buy my (stupid) tickets.

He said, *That's nonsense, Kim. Plenty of people will buy your tickets—you just have to change your approach and control the sale.*

"Control the sale" to an 8-year-old boy? Really?

He saw the dumb look on my face to that comment, so he explained that I just needed to get their attention by asking a question right away that was easier to answer with a yes than a no. Not a question impossible to say no to, just one to which it would be easier to answer with a yes.

I offered him another dumb look.

He thought for a moment and then told me to ask this question to the person who opens the door, *Do you believe in the Boy Scouts of America?* He said just about everyone would say yes to that question, especially coming from a cute 8-year-old boy. (And I was cute, too.) He added that if anyone said no to just walk away without another word because anyone who didn't believe in the Boy Scouts was a jerk who wouldn't want the tickets if I gave them away.

There were only three days left in the contest, and I was way behind the leader. Desperate things call for serious action, so the very next day after school I put on my Cub Scout uniform, grabbed a hand full of tickets, and hit the street, ready to put my dad's sales lesson to the test and win that 10-Speed.

At the very first door I knocked, a young mother opened the door with a smile and greeted me with a friendly, "Yes?"

I did exactly what my dad told me to do. I looked her right in the eye and asked the Big Question. *Do you believe in the Boy Scouts of America?*

She continued to smile and answered without hesitation, *Of course I do.*

Then, thrilled she was following my dad's script and that I had her attention, I immediately followed up with the control comment and hard close that my dad told me to say, *Then I'm sure you'll support us by buying tickets to the upcoming Boy Scouts Fun-O-Rama…How many do you want?*

A hard close from a little boy in a Cub Scout uniform can be a bit disconcerting. Her smile dropped a bit, and she gave me a weird look, but I just stood there and smiled. After a moment of strained silence, she held up two fingers, smiled, and said, *I'll take two.*

I had just sold two tickets and at the very first door on which I knocked! Wow! My dad was a genius!

I followed that exact process for the last three days of the contest and my sales skyrocketed! A couple of jerks said "no" to my question about the Boy Scouts, and I just walked away. But almost everyone I met said "yes" and bought at least one ticket. WOW!

My rise in the final three days was nothing short of meteoric, but the hole I'd dug with the eleven prior days of poor sales was just too deep to climb out of and I did not win the bicycle. I don't think the loss caused me any permanent emotional damage (well…not much, anyway), but I did come in 2nd place, and I did win something pretty cool. Plus, I avoided the shame of just getting a crappy ribbon.

The little boy who came in 1st and won the bicycle and the little boy who came in right behind me at 3rdplace, each had an army of relatives pestering everyone and their dog to buy tickets to help their little boy. The point of this story is that I didn't have that army of relatives helping me. I made all of those sales myself. Just me. An eight-year-old boy knocking on doors using a sales process taught to me by my dad.

That sales lesson my dad gave me when I was a small boy lies at the very foundation of everything there is to know regarding sales in general and specifically, selling anything door-to-door. To wit: guide the conversation and control the sale by asking questions and making comments that are easier to answer with a yes than a no. Period. It's not rocket science. It's sales.

Fast forward a few decades to when I was struggling to find a process to consistently start more conversations at the door so that I could sell cable TV subscriptions and earn a consistent, high-level income. Suddenly, my dad's simple lesson from when I was a kid came back to me like a couple of hard slaps to the back of my head. WACK! And a moment later another, WACK!

In a moment of clarity created by the 1st hard mental slap, I realized that I was saying things at the door that were not easier to answer positively with a yes than a no, but instead, I was saying things in my Opening At The Door that practically **invited** the prospect to say **no** and turn me away. Good grief. I was doing the opposite of what my dad taught me when I was a boy. I was shooting myself in the foot. Bad move...

The 2nd hard mental slap drove me to realize that I needed to stop trying to sell my products at the door as part of my opening. Cable had more moving parts than simple tickets to a Boy Scout event, so I needed to treat the Opening At The Door as a totally separate sale in and of itself. I needed to sell the prospect on wanting to have a conversation with me about my products so that I could then sell the products. Okay. Getting better...

Think about it. The price a prospect pays for a brief conversation is just a few minutes of their time. Whereas the price they pay to buy products and services is their hard-earned cash. Ergo, selling a conversation should be an easier sale to make. Right? And since people who buy one thing from you are inclined to also buy something else from you, then when the prospect bites on your opening and buys the conversation, you will be in a very strong position to make a successful second sale of your products because you have a receptive prospect. Bingo. Money in the bank.

I re-tooled my thought process and applied the consultative sales process to selling a **conversation** at the door instead of trying to sell my stuff. When I made that change, my sales took off. Really. Those two hard mental slaps drove me to concentrate and create a simple yet effective Opening At The Door Sales Process (OATD) that enabled me to consistently sell the conversation to get past the door so that I could then sell my actual product(s) and earn fat commissions.

A lot has changed in the cable industry since I began. Cable operators have grown from just video antennas into full-fledged communications companies that offer multiple platforms and services, often including non-cable services like home security, mobile phone service, and more. Competition has also increased to the point where satellite services have tens of millions of subscribers and many areas of the country also have hard-line operators that overlap and compete against each other and satellite for customers. Any area where satellite and multiple hardline operators compete against each other makes for very stiff competition. To be a star, you have to become and remain a sales pro. Period. And that all starts with the Opening At The Door.

Starting a sales conversation with someone who doesn't know you exist until they open their door is the most important part of the process because, again, you can't close a sale you can't start. I steadily adapted my Opening At The Door Sales (OATD) process to where it is now a five-step system that **any rep selling any product or service can adapt** and make it their own.

To fully understand why my OATD works as well as it does, let me first offer important facts about the job to help you get people to want to speak with you about what you sell. These bits of knowledge are the building blocks upon which you can adapt and customize my five-step process so that you can start more conversations that lead to bigger and better sales.

Six Critical Facts About Getting Past the Door

Fact #1—Make Two Sales

It is a fact that today you need to close two sales to earn one commission. Since you can't close a sale that you can't first start, the first sale you need to make is to sell the prospect on **wanting to have a conversation with you** about your products and services. As I mentioned earlier, the price paid by the prospect for the conversation is simply a few minutes of their time. Whereas the price they pay for your products and services is their hard-earned cash.

Too often I see sales reps miss the boat entirely by trying to sell their products and services right off the bat as their **opening** instead of breaking the process into two sales, with the close of the first leading into the start of the second. Start the sale with your opening, next sell your products and services by following the professional consultative sales process of uncovering needs, presenting, and closing.

Fact #2—People are Suspicious

It is a fact that prospects greet you with suspicion when they open their door. Some say it out loud and with varying degrees of politeness. *Who are you and why are you on my porch?* But thankfully, most just ask that question in their head. The best way to get past the suspicion and start a sales conversation is to immediately present yourself as a professional looking to HELP instead of a stranger simply trying to make a SALE.

Fact #3—Control the Sale

It is a fact that successful sales professionals are able to comfortably and conversationally gain and maintain control of the sales conversation from start to finish, all the way from when the prospect opens the door to when you walk out the door with a signed contract.

One way they do this is by using a technique I call **ANSWER ASK**. This means, in short, that every time you answer a question or respond to a comment by the prospect, that you end your response or comment with another question of your own. Hence the term, ANSWER ASK. Always ending with a question eliminates **dead air** and compels the prospect to answer and therefore, stay engaged in the conversation. To use high-speed Internet service as an example, a sales professional responds to a question about Internet speeds with an answer and finishes the response with an open-ended question to pull the prospect further into the conversation while potentially uncovering buyer needs...*Good question, Mr. Prospect. We offer speeds from a hundred megs up to a gig...what all do you now have connected to the Internet?*

Fact #4—Not Just a Numbers Game

It is a fact that to be successful, which to me means to make enough sales to achieve your sales goals and earn a very good living, a significant portion of your sales need to come from people who are **happy with what they already have** from the competition when you meet them. Of course, you will occasionally come across people who are not happy with what they have from your competitor for whatever reason...poor customer service, billing issues, service outages, too many rats and roaches...whatever, and these should all be easy sales to make. However, you **cannot** be successful (see above) just selling to these people. Amateurs who barely earn a living just play the numbers game of quantity door knocking and a *give me your no quickly so I can get that out of the way and keep looking for the yes from the next person* attitude. Finding people at home is tough enough in this job, so be a professional and take advantage of every contact you make. When I was a commission-only salesman, the average sales to contact ratio of most members of the team was only one closed sale for every 20 contacts – that's only 5%. Mine was 10+ closed sales out of 20 contacts or 50%. Plus, I created a clever technique to generate sales later on from the remaining 50% of contacts that I could not sell at the time. I named that technique **NAME/NUMBER,** and I'll share it with you later on.

To earn a good living in today's competitive environment, you need to be able to start the conversation with someone who is happy with what they've already got, and once the conversation is started, use the consultative sales process to guide these same people into seeing, all on their own, that what you have is a better value for them—that what they really want is your stuff. It is called **sales**. And in today's competitive marketplace everyone in direct sales must be able to **sell**.

Fact #5—Same Side of the Door

It is a fact that both you and the prospect need to be on the same side of the door threshold with the door closed to your back with you inside or to the prospect's back with them outside **before** you begin your sales conversation about your products and services.

The reasons are many...more comfortable inside or perhaps the prospect's house is a mess and they prefer to speak outside, and of course, in areas of extreme hot or cold weather, the longer the prospect holds the door open the more their heat or air-conditioned air escapes which costs them money, and most people do not look favorably upon salespeople who cost them money. Hence, the need to be on the same side of the door before you try to sell your stuff.

Fact #6—Offer Benefit to Sell the Conversation

It is a fact that you need to give the people who open their door a benefit to speaking with you to sell a conversation. People buy benefits, and you are selling a conversation, so give them something to buy and offer at least one terrific benefit to speaking with you.

To identify the selling benefit to use in your opening, try to concisely answer the very important question prospects need answered...*What's in it for me?* Don't be glib or pushy. Be calm and friendly and offer a compelling benefit to speaking with you more.

Good Sales Communication

With the facts about two sales in mind, here are some critical points that will further contextualize my OATD process.

Point #1 is to be clear about who you are and what you represent. Do not try to hide the fact you are a salesperson but instead, come right out and admit you're a salesperson and then do everything in your power to not fulfill the common negative stereotype about door-to-door salespeople—that we are all pushy and aggressive and willing to tell any lie to make a sale.

Point #2 is to be positive, upbeat, and attentive. Project a positive presence at every door on which you knock and with every conversation you have. Remember that your job is to help people get a better value with your product and your service than they currently receive with your competitor, and that is something to be upbeat and positive about. Keep in mind that your attitude is noticeable right off the bat by people who open that door. So be positive. This also applies when you are walking from one door to another. Wave and smile at everyone you see in the neighborhood you work as they walk or drive by. This small yet personal touch will make them more likely to engage with you when you knock on their door. You are on stage the minute you get to the territory. People will notice you in their neighborhood so make every impression friendly and professional.

Point #3 is to be concise. I cannot reiterate enough that trying to sell your services instead of a conversation at the door takes time and immediately illustrates to the prospect that you are a salesman trying to sell them something that they probably don't want. Bang. Bang. Two shots to the feet. The opening process I created takes no more than 12 or 15 seconds to deliver and clearly illustrates that you are a professional who will not waste their valuable time trying to get them to buy something they don't want. Clear, positive, and concise is good sales communication at the door.

The Opening At The Door: Five-Step Proven Process to Get Past the Door

My professional Opening At The Door is the best there is to consistently start cold-call sales conversations at the door in today's hot, competitive marketplace. Although it has proven itself to be singularly effective for selling cable TV subscriptions and pest controls services, it can easily be adapted to start cold-call sales conversations for solar panels, landscape services, or just about anything that can be sold door-to-door— even meat. (Yes, I did get approached by a door-to-door salesman selling meat. He was good, and I bought some.)

I have been in the cable TV industry for decades so I will use those products and services to 'fill in the blanks' in the illustrations of the process. Additionally, as a sales trainer, I have coached many pest control agents on how to start their cold-call sales process and have seen first-hand how my opening process has helped them boost both the quantity and quality of their sales, so I will also offer an example of how my process works for those services.

Starting a good sales conversation at the door takes only 12-15 seconds and follows this Five-Step Process:

1. Gain control.
2. Greet and identify yourself with your name, job title, and company.
3. Offer a **feature**—tell them why you are on their porch.

4. Offer a **benefit** to speaking with you because people buy benefits and not features, and you are looking to sell a conversation.

5. Close the sale of the conversation.

Before Step 1, start with the obvious. Walk up to the door, knock, and practice good body language as previously outlined. Keep both hands in plain view, holding your clipboard or tablet and of course, with your company ID visible and a sincere smile on your face.

Step #1: Gain Control

Smile as the prospect opens the door and **hand them something** to look at **as you begin to speak**. A business card, a channel lineup or a brochure about your company will do. Anything will work as the 'gain control' mechanism as long as what you hand them has your name and contact information on it and **does not have any prices on it**. You want them to be able to reach you in the future, and you do not want to shoot yourself in the foot by mentioning the price of anything before you've sold the conversation—even in print!

This action to take control accomplishes three things:

1. It puts you in control of the encounter because the prospect does something you want them to do. You offer and they accept your handout.

2. It takes some pressure off of you having to be perfect with your opening because they look at what you hand them and are not staring at some stranger on their porch. They take it and look at it as you speak and as long as there are no prices on what you hand them, they will listen to what you say.

3. It legitimizes you as a professional who is safe to interact with. Everything about you should convey professionalism and security. Handing them something from your company builds some trust.

Step #2: Greet and Identify Yourself with Your Name, Job Title, and Company

As they accept your handout, say your name, job title, and company name. For a cable TV rep it is: *Hi, I'm Kim, the* **DISTRICT** *sales rep and* **MEDIA EXPERT** *for this area with* (name of your company).

For pest control I say, *Hi, I'm Kim, the* **DISTRICT** *sales rep and* **PEST ELIMINATION EXPERT** *for this area with* (name of your company).

When normal people see someone on their porch with a clipboard or tablet wearing some kind of company garment and ID, they assume that person is selling something. They most often make assumptions, mostly negative, right away about that person that stand in the way of having a further conversation. Even though they are set to 'just say no' when they open the door, if the sales rep calmly and professionally admits s/he is a salesperson, then the salesperson gains a modicum of trust for being upfront and honest, both of which are very positive.

Notice your modern job title is both **DISTRICT SALES REP** and **MEDIA EXPERT**. The former because you are a salesperson and by admitting it upfront, you combat the common negative stereotype that door-to-door salespeople are sneaky and untrustworthy. You gain a small bit of trust with this confession so don't waste it. Putting **DISTRICT** at the front implies that you are higher up the corporate ladder than just the common frontline door-to-door sales schmo, which also helps a great deal with perception. You have now gained trust points for being honest and for having a cool title. Adding **MEDIA EXPERT** at the end of your cool job title lets the prospect know right away that you know what you are talking about and can answer any questions they may have regarding their media services. Same with **PEST ELIMINATION EXPERT** for pest control. Regular people will think, *Wow, this guy knows how to kill bugs!*

Most people prefer to deal with an expert, so be one. I have personally found that adding MEDIA EXPERT/ PEST ELIMINATION EXPERT to my job title works wonders in high-end areas at selling the conversation because most middle-class and affluent people are not willing to give you their time unless you bring value and expertise to the conversation. Being an EXPERT adds to the value you bring to the conversational party.

Please note that **how** you deliver each word and line of the opening is critical to success. Your mother was right when she said *It's not what you say but how you say it that counts* in response to some snarky comment you made to her when you were a teenager. So follow what your mother told you and accentuate the power words and phrases I put in **BOLD** because how you say them increases their effectiveness. Drive them home with the tone—not volume, but the tone—of your voice. Just say everything else in your normal voice.

No one wants to listen to a monotone ramble so practice speaking with clarity and conviction. Practice the opening to the point of being dramatic (really) so that you truly accentuate the power words to make them stand out. Through your opening, use your hands as you speak for additional punctuation and emphasis. *Hi, I'm Kim, the* **DISTRICT** *sales rep and* **MEDIA EXPERT** *for this area with the local cable company.* (I use my free arm to make a sweeping motion indicating 'this area.')

At this point, it has taken you only about five seconds to take control of the conversation and tell the prospect that you are a salesperson with a big title and extra skills. Now it's time to offer them a feature and tell them why you are there.

Step #3: Offer a Feature—Tell Them Why You Are on Their Porch

*Hi, I'm Kim the **DISTRICT** sales rep and **MEDIA EXPERT** for this area with your local cable company... And I am out here tonight looking for people **WHO I CAN HELP...***

This line is not unlike getting junk mail that says *You may already be a winner!* I always open those to see what I may have already won, knowing full well that it is just a pitch. But, hey, maybe this time I really will win something! So, like junk mail, when a person hears this line, they may subconsciously think, *Hmmm, I wonder if he can help me?* You now have their attention, and a lot of the initial negative assumptions change for the better, and the prospect is set up to be receptive to the next thing you say. Which, as people buy benefits and you are selling a sales conversation, will be a benefit the prospect will gain by hearing more of what you have to say...So give the prospect something to buy.

At this point, it has taken you only about eight or nine seconds to take control of the conversation. Now—tell the prospect that you are a salesperson with a big title and extra skills, and let them know that you are looking for specific people who you can help.

Step #4: Offer a Benefit Linked Directly to the Help You Are Looking to Provide

This part of the opening should be specific to the product you sell, and as best as possible, to the area you are in. For cable TV reps, use a broad brush regarding your service offerings and stress the power word **VALUE**. For example: *And I am out here tonight looking for people who I can help gain a* **MUCH BETTER VALUE EVERY MONTH** *with their* **MEDIA SERVICES...**

If you are working in an area that's on the lower end of the economic spectrum, try the blunt approach of **SAVING MONEY**. For example: *And I am out here tonight looking for people who I can help* **SAVE MONEY EVERY MONTH** *on their* **MEDIA SERVICES...** As a rule, **VALUE** carries more weight with people who have larger disposable incomes, and **SAVING MONEY** carries more weight in the areas where every dollar counts.

I strongly recommend against ever mentioning a specific dollar amount in your opening that the prospect may save because you just don't know until you make the sale and see what the net result is. I say this because I know from firsthand experience that a prospect will take as a promise any specific dollar amount you mention in your opening, and if at the end of the sales process you can't deliver on that 'promised amount,' then you come across as dishonest and your sale falls into a hole you can't climb out of. No sale. Better luck next time. **MUCH BETTER VALUE** and **SAVE**

MONEY (without a dollar amount) are powerful but also fairly nebulous so they get the prospect's attention without creating any kind of perceived promise.

Another way for a cable TV sales rep to offer a benefit that works well in today's super-connected world: *And I am out here tonight looking for people who I can* **HELP**... *gain a much* **FASTER** *and* **MORE RELIABLE HIGH-SPEED INTERNET SERVICE** *than they currently have*... With "faster and more reliable Internet" being the benefit.

A good benefit a pest control rep can offer is **peace of mind**. So the opening to this point is: *And I am out here tonight looking for people* **WHO I CAN HELP** *gain the* **PEACE OF MIND** *of knowing* **OBNOXIOUS** *and* **POSSIBLY DANGEROUS PESTS** *will not threaten or harm their family*...

At this point, it has taken you only **about 12 seconds** to take control of the conversation. You admit to the prospect that you are a salesperson but with a big title and extra skills and let them know that you are looking for specific people (those you can help) and offering those specific people (how you can help them) a good reason to speak with you more.

Step #5: Close the Sale of the Conversation

The last step of your Opening At The Door is to close the sale of the conversation so that both you and the prospect are together on the same side of the threshold with the door closed—either to your back because you are inside the dwelling, or to the prospect's back because s/he is outside with you.

The 1st four steps of the opening for cable reps that we've covered to this point are: Speak as you extend your hand with something that has your name and number on it for the prospect to hold...*Hi, I'm Kim, the* **DISTRICT** *sales rep and* **MEDIA EXPERT** *for this area with ABC cable, and I am out here tonight looking for people* **WHO I CAN HELP** *gain* **A MUCH BETTER VALUE EVERY MONTH** *with their* **MEDIA SERVICES...**

The 1st four steps of the opening for a pest control sales rep are: Speak as you extend your hand with something with your name and number on it for the prospect to hold *Hi, I'm Kim, the* **DISTRICT** *sales rep and* **PEST ELIMINATION EXPERT** *for this area with* ABC Bug Killers, *And I am out here tonight looking for people* **WHO I CAN HELP** *gain the* **PEACE OF MIND** *of knowing* **OBNOXIOUS** *and* **POSSIBLY DANGEROUS PESTS** *will not threaten or harm their family...*

Step five of the OATD process is to effectively close the sale of a conversation. Offer a very brief (one second) pause after you offer the benefit (the WIIFM) and then close the sale by asking the open-ended closing question, ***Where's a good place for us to sit down?***

Remember my Cub Scout story from earlier? The success of the entire pitch and the reason I *almost* won the 10-speed was because I asked a question in my opening that was easier to answer with a positive than a negative. Not impossible, simply easier. The absolute same process applies here. The open-ended question of *Where's a good place for us to sit down?* is not an easy question to just say NO to because it is an open question, and open questions cannot easily be answered with just one word. Open-ended questions beg a response, and when used as the close, you will often find their response to be (I kid you not) *How about my kitchen?* Ka-Boom! You are inside their house and about to launch into the sale of your services to earn a commission.

Alternatively, if they don't invite you inside and, let's face it, **most won't**, they may ask a question relating to your opening, your company, or your product. If they do, which **many will**, then acknowledge the question and offer a brief and accurate reply and once again ask to come inside. For example, the prospect may ask, *What's a media expert?* Acknowledge, respond and close again with: *Good question. I received additional training to ensure that every customer I help receives only what they want and that they know how everything works.* (Insert one second pause) *Where's a good place for us to sit down?*

The most common problem I face with reps in my workshops is that they want to change the open-ended closing question into a closed-ended question. Instead of asking, *Where's a good place for us to sit down?* they ask, *Is there a place where we can sit down?* Or *Can we sit somewhere to discuss?*

Do not ask this as a closed-ended question because such phrasing makes it **easier for the prospect to say no** and turn you away. *Is there a place where we can* *sit down?* Practically invites the prospect to respond with, *No. I'm good thanks. Goodbye...*and you've shot yourself in the foot and you are done. Better luck next time.

But with the open-ended version, *where's a good place for us to sit down?* Just saying no is awkward and therefore not easy for most people to do. Not impossible by any means, just not easy, and since sales follow the path of least resistance, every time you make it easier for the prospect to say yes than no, the more yesses you will hear and the more sales you will make.

Hi, I'm Kim, the **DISTRICT** *sales rep and* **MEDIA EXPERT** *for this area with ABC cable, and I am out here tonight* **LOOKING FOR PEOPLE WHO I CAN HELP** *get a much better* **VALUE** *every month with their* **MEDIA SERVICES**...*Where's a good place for us to sit down?*

I occasionally get push-back in my workshops from sales reps who don't want to ask for a good place to sit down. Okay. So change it to *chat,* or *to have a brief conversation.* The key to starting the conversation is to **always finish your opening with an open-ended question** because such a question is easier to answer with a positive than a negative. Remember that the sales process for your services **begins when the door is closed**, either to your back with you inside or to the prospect's back with them outside.

With the brief pause before the close, this opening should only take about 15 seconds, and when delivered properly, it will consistently start good cold-call sales conversations.

The Opening At The Door for MDU Sales Reps

The Opening At The Door for a Multiple Dwelling Unit (MDU) sales rep who needs to cold-call residents of a property assigned to them, is essentially the same as for single-family reps, but with a simple edit in Step 1 of the process where you identify yourself. In an MDU, add *for this complex* to your job title.

Perception is everything in sales communication. And being specific about that property can elevate the perception of your expertise and importance in the grand scheme of things to the prospect. The more a prospect sees you as an expert, the higher they will hold you in regard, and the easier it will be to start a sales conversation. *Hi, I'm Kim, the **district** sales rep and **media expert for this complex** with your local cable company, and I am out looking for residents **who I can help** get a much **better value every month** on their media services...**Where's** a good place for us to sit down?*

Practice Makes Perfect

It is a fact that starting the conversation is the most critical step in the process. The first 12 to 15 seconds at the door has everything to do with making money, so you should strive to deliver your opening as comfortably and naturally as possible. You gain comfort by practicing. Create your opening according to the Five-step formula I just presented, and then practice it a zillion times so that you sound natural and not robotic or "salesy." Do not blow this off with a quick *I got this* and just practice it as you use it in the field. Get it down pat before you take it to the field.

Professionals practice to stay sharp in any discipline and door-to-door sales is no exception. For example, if you show up at a major league baseball game a couple of hours before game time, you will see the players practicing their skills. These select few men can play baseball at the highest level possible and have been playing the sport practically all their lives, yet they still practice every day before a game because their income depends on how well they play the game. Even when they've made the major leagues, they still practice daily. Practicing is crucial.

Considerably less glamorous than professional sports, but the same fact applies in door-to-door sales. Your income depends entirely upon making sales, and you can't close a sale you can't first start. Think of the prospect opening the door as the first pitch you'll see at the plate. The more practice you take before that plate appearance, the more comfortable you will be taking your swing. Hit it squarely with a good and comfortable opening, and you're in the game. Stumble or come across poorly and you're OUT on Strike one. Go to the next door.

I had a new hire in a workshop some years ago who was in his late 20s. He had a high school education and had never earned more than minimum wage. He wanted to do better in his life, so he took a job as a door-to-door salesman for the local cable company. I was under contract with that company to train their new hires, so he attended my in-person, 2-day sales training course. His name was Tom, and he was physically imposing, but not in a good way. To be blunt, he was tall, very overweight, and kind of scary looking. But all that aside, he paid attention during the training. He wanted to make good money, and he focused like a laser beam on learning how to do the job.

I am delighted to say that he went out after training and used my Opening At The Door to start conversations and get inside the house, and he made sales. His looks didn't slow him down in the slightest (nor should anyone's), and he did so well right off the bat that his first paycheck was by far the largest single paycheck he had ever received! I was proud of him, but more importantly, he was proud of himself.

Three months after training he called me up in a panic. He said he needed a new Opening At The Door because that one I taught him in my training simply wasn't working anymore. I asked him to role play so that I could hear the opening he was using, but he pushed back, insisting that he was saying **exactly what I taught him to say at the door.** After repeated requests he finally relented to role play and here is exactly how it went:

Me to Tom, as the prospect opening the door: *Hello?*

Tom to me, the prospect: ***Hi I'm Tom let me in!***

Me to Tom: *Tom. I think I see the problem.*

Turns out Tom was like countless other sales reps who do well at first, so they think they've got it down and they don't practice. This causes them to get off track just a bit, so they make a small change to get back on track, which doesn't help much, so they make another small change that takes them even further off track... and just like that they have deviated far from the proven process they learned and are once again simply playing the numbers game and making it up as they go along.

The OATD I offer in this book has been tested thousands of times and is proven to be the most effective opening there is to consistently start cold-call sales conversations with people who don't know you from Adam until they open their door and meet you on their porch. But the OATD is much more than the specific words. To hit the pitch and knock it out of the park, you need to incorporate the subtle voice changes and body language moves I recommend, which makes it perfect. But that requires practice.

Overcoming Common Objections at the Door

I make getting inside the house sound so easy, don't I? Well, it would be if everyone was open, friendly, and receptive to speaking with someone they just met on their porch! But that isn't the case many times—regardless of how well you deliver your opening, the prospect will still say NO and turn you away. These at-the-door objections range from the immediate rude—*GO AWAY!* punctuated with a door slam (I hate those guys.), to the polite response where the prospect waits until after your pitch to then say, *No thank you. I'm happy with what I've got,* or *Not interested,* or *No thanks, I'm good* as they move to close their door. Whichever it is, they are giving you the brush off. They are objecting to your attempt to sell a sales conversation. Objections are part and parcel to sales and objections at the door are the most common in the entire door-to-door sales experience and you have to get past them to sell the conversation.

Zig Ziglar said that a sale is made every time. Either they buy what you're selling (which at this point is a conversation) or you buy their no. Do not buy their no at the door and just walk away. Many, many times just one good attempt to get past their objection is all it takes to get the sale on track. And if you want to make a ton of money at this job—and you bought this book, so I know you do—then if your 'one good attempt' doesn't work. Try a 2nd good attempt, a 3rd attempt, and so on until they either let you in or they are about to get mad (at which point you take their name and number for a follow-up call later on). I will show you how to get a prospect who is stuck on NO to willingly give you their name and number. It truly works, and you'll love it!

The point of clarification is if the person is flat-out rude, crude or insulting then walk away. They are not saying NO they are just being jerks, and jerks don't count. Keep your spirits up and smile and walk away and assume the next door will be opened by a warm and friendly person. The good news is that true jerks are rare. If the person who opens the door is not a jerk and doesn't just slam the door in your face (a typical jerk move) then you have a shot.

Sometimes people say NO to give themselves a minute to decide whether you are worth talking to so continue being a professional to assure them that you are. Do this: First, **Acknowledge** the fact they made an objection (*Okay. I get that…I hear you…*) and then respond using either *If I can, will you?* Or, *Feel, felt, found* to overcome their objection and then confirm you did get past it by repeating the open-ended question/ request to come inside. *Where's a good place for us to sit down?* **Always** finish your attempt to overcome any and all objections at the door with the open-ended question/request to come inside. They are voicing an objection to a conversation, not to the sale of your services. So do not get all wordy but follow the KISS formula and Keep It Simple, Stupid.

A typical objection is, *No thanks. I am happy with what I've got.* You will hear this because your competitor has good products, and people are happy with them. Here are three ways to overcome and get past this objection:

If I can, will you?

*I get that. Our competitors have good products. But **if I can** show you how you can get a much better value every month with our services, **will you** speak with me? Where's a good place for us to sit down?*

Feel, Felt, Found

*I get that. I know how you **feel** because our competitors have good products. And many of my customers **felt** the same way, but they **found** after speaking with me that I could offer them a much better **value** every month. Where's a good place for us to sit down?*

*Or I know how you **feel**, and your neighbor **felt** the same way, but when they switched to our better, faster service they **found** they liked us a lot more than what they had. Where's a good place for us to sit down?*

Acknowledge and Respond

I get that. Our competitors have good products, but our products are better, and as the District Sales Rep, I can get you a better value every month than what you now have. Where's a good place for us to sit down?

The key is to always **acknowledge** that they made an objection, offer a **brief** response, and **ask again** for the sale of the conversation.

3

Name/Number

*How to turn the no at the door
into a yes later on...*

Sometimes the prospect is just stuck on NO. Even though you do an excellent job of delivering your OATD and make at least a couple of strong tries at overcoming their no to keep the sales process moving forward, the prospect sticks with no and you're done. Bummer. On to the next door, right?

Not so fast.

Assuming the prospect isn't a rude jerk (in which case you simply walk away because life's too short to deal with jerks), you still might sell to that person if you can get them to *willingly* give you their name and phone number so that you can make a follow-up call later on and catch them, hopefully, in a more receptive mood. The trick is for them to **willingly** give you their name and number at their door after they have repeatedly said no.

I developed a process that truly works in getting the prospect to give you their name and number—regardless of how emphatic their objection was to your OATD. Really. It works.

The first part of the process is to know when to stop trying to sell the conversation. As a salesman, you want to be assertive. You need to be assertive. But there is a big difference between being assertive and being overly aggressive (a jerk). So when someone says no, and you fail to get past their no with your rebuttals, then you need to stop trying before they get angry. Because if you continue until they get genuinely pissed, then they will never buy anything from you, and that's not good. Especially if you have a territory to develop. So when you get to the point where you see them starting to get pissed, stop talking. Just stop. Pause. Smile. And then get their name and phone number for a follow-up call as you leave.

Here is how you get them to willingly give you their name and number. It is as simple as this. Just say two words to them with a brief pause in the middle: Name...Number. But you need to put in a small touch of drama to make it work.

Here's the process...You push a couple of times to get passed their NO using one or more of the verbal tools I mentioned earlier, but the tools aren't working and you see the prospect starting to get pissed at your assertiveness, so you stop. Smile and acknowledge their NO with a simple and polite apology. Something like, *I understand. I don't mean to be pushy. You have my contact information* (because it is on the handout you gave them when they opened the door). *Please call me if you change your mind.* And then you physically **turn your body and begin to walk away**. But when you are halfway turned around and your body is perpendicular to their door, **stop moving your body,** but turn your head to face them and then, all in one motion, briefly **lock eyes** (Super brief. It's not a stare down) **as you point at them with your pen**, and then **pull your eyes and your pen down** to something to write on as you say, **do not ask**, **but say, name...number**. Keep your eyes looking down at what you are writing on with your pen poised above the surface and wait for them to speak. They will give it to you. Really. The more you do it exactly as I describe, the more successful you will be. **Do not ask**...*will you please give me your name and phone number?* Because they will say no every time. I mean, why would they say yes? They are telling you no at the door, so why on Earth would they want to give you their number so that you can call them later to make a sales pitch. Duh.

But if you follow my directions and actually begin to turn away, then no matter how much they were beginning to think of you as a jerk because you were being assertive and not accepting their no, if you smile, offer a brief apology, and begin to turn away they will think better of you at that moment. They will think, *All right. This guy isn't so bad. He is giving up. I pushed the salesman away. I WIN!* That is the moment to stop moving, lock eyes as you point at them with your pen, and then pull both your eyes and your pen down to your pad as you say *Name...Number*. Do not look at them, just keep looking at your pad. This action pulls it out of them, and they will tell you both their name and their phone number. I guarantee it will work.

Write down their name and number and walk away. I recommend rating them as potential sales depending upon how they were in their *No*. From a polite, *I just don't have time right now* kind-of-no, to a forceful *I hate your company kind-of-no*. The former you want to call within 48 hours and the latter after a few days. But call them both.

This works! You see...when you are at somebody's door and they say no to your approach and no to all attempts at rebuttal, their *no* could be based on a number of factors that have nothing to do with you, your product, or your company. You don't know what's going on in their lives when you stop by. Maybe the kids are blowing up, or maybe they are just about to leave. You don't know. But if you get their name and number and call them in a day or two, those factors that drove them to say *no* to you at the door may have passed. Plus, when you call them later, it will be a **warm call because they met you on their porch**. For good or ill, you are no longer a stranger.

When you call them later, be brief and remind them where you met. *Hi Mr. Prospect, this is Kim from Smash 'em Dead bug killers. We met the other day on your porch...* Keep the call brief because, just like at the door, you are selling an appointment to come by. You are not selling your products or services. So use a hook to get them to want to speak with you in person and ask for a time to come by.

If they ask after they give you their name and number what you want it for, just mention you will follow up later to see if they would be interested in **taking advantage** of any of the terrific offers you will have at that time as you walk away.

Then leave and go to the next door.

I have made countless sales using this process from people who initially turn me away at the door. It works.

4

Uncovering Buyer Needs

Tell me why you want to buy my stuff...

You sold the conversation so now it's time to sell your products by first finding out what kind and how many needs the prospect has for what you sell. This step is called, cleverly enough, Uncovering Buyer Needs and it lies at the very heart of the Consultative Sales Process.

This step is critical because if you don't first uncover the needs before you present to make the sale, then you are trying to make a **push sale** by just asking the prospect to buy your stuff. *Here's what I've got and here's how much it cost. Do you wanna buy it?* If they already wanted it when they met you, then you might make a sale, but in many cases, that sale will be for far less than it could be, so you will be leaving money on the table.

It is a sales truth that **everybody likes to buy, but nobody likes to be sold**. This truth illustrates why the consultative approach is so effective because it shows us in a step-by-step manner, how to **guide** prospects into seeing all on their own that what we offer is something they **want** to buy…then we just help them make the purchase. They get what they want, and we earn a commission. Bingo.

The content I cover in this chapter and for the rest of this book are advanced sales skills that are used by **successful** sales professionals everywhere to sell anything and everything. It is the consultative approach where, just as the word implies, the salesperson (you) *consults* with the prospect to ensure s/he buys exactly what s/he wants, as opposed to the push, push, push style of selling where the salesperson (hopefully **not** you) does not consult, but instead, does everything possible to push the prospect into purchasing what the salesperson wants to sell.

The First Four Steps of the Consultative Sales Process

The **Consultative Sales Process** has eight steps. **The first four steps get us past the door** and into an effective sales conversation. They are:

1. Relate
2. Question
3. Listen
4. Acknowledge

Relate means establishing a rapport with the prospect and starting the conversation. For you, this is your Opening At The Door, which I just covered in length. You can't close what you can't start so you have to establish a rapport with the person who opens the door to have any hope of making a sale. Every word you choose to use during the opening will either inspire somebody to talk to you or convince them not to have the conversation. Choose your words wisely when you fill in the blanks of your opening. Then practice in the mirror and with selfie videos to ensure you get the right cadence and emphasis to look, act, and sound like a friendly, but serious professional.

The next three steps are **Question, Listen** and **Acknowledge.** To be consistently successful in selling any product or service, you have to first determine *why* anyone would want to own what you sell. Come up with a list of as many reasons as possible someone would like to own what you sell, and then, armed with that knowledge, you use these three steps of the process to comfortably and conversationally see if your prospect's **needs, wants, and possibilities** overlap with the **whys** on your list. Every time you hear an overlap, regardless of how small, that is a reason for them to want to buy what you sell. So uncover **as many needs as possible** (AMNAP for short) so that you can find as many overlaps as possible. The more overlaps of their expressed needs to the benefits of owning what you sell, the easier and the better the sale.

I'll go over each step of these three critical steps individually, and then I'll share with you the formula of how they work in concert to set up for **the best sale possible**. But first, let me show you how to uncover needs right away while avoiding falling into the trap of **The Salesman Dance.**

The first opportunity to uncover buyer needs often occurs right on the porch when the prospect appears to bite on your opening by cutting to the chase and asking right out, *What's your best deal?* When this happens (and it does a lot), most sales reps assume the prospect will buy once they hear **their super offer,** and they mentally put the commission money in their pocket. The problematic trap here is that if you take the bait and start throwing out packages and prices in answer to their question, you will most likely fail because hearing the prospect ask for your *best deal* does not mean they want anything you've got. Not at all because **no needs** for your products have been identified. Lots of times people ask that question just to see the salesman dance. And the rep is left on the porch with a big WTF look on his/her face after the prospect listens for a moment and then says, *no thanks* and closes the door.

Do not do the salesman dance of verbally vomiting up different packages, bundles, and offers simply because the prospect asks for them during your opening. Instead, use their question to gain control of the conversation and keep the sale moving forward as you portray yourself as a true professional while getting inside the house.

Say this: *I am the district sales rep, so I have a lot of great deals/offers,* (micro brief pause to let that line sink in, then add) *but so that I do not waste your time talking about something you don't want, please tell me what you have now in the way of digital video, high-speed internet access, and telephone service.* (micro pause with a big smile with hand outstretched and palm face up) *Where's a good place for us to sit down?*

If you sell pest control change the middle part to... *please tell me what you have now in the way of how you keep your family safe from noxious pests...where's a good place for us to sit down?*

By starting it with **I have a lot of great deals,** (or offers, whichever you are more comfortable using) you let the prospect know that he or she will have choices, and by continuing with **so that I don't waste your time talking about something you don't want**...You tell the person that you are not there to push anything down their throat, which may gain you some respect. And by finishing with **Where's a good place for us to sit down** you are again trying to close the sale of the conversation (Relate) by asking to come inside. The entire response supports the image of you being an expert trying to help and not a pushy salesperson trying to push them into buying what you've got.

For those people who do not toss out an invitation to see The Salesman Dance and let you inside or come outside to be with you, the sale of your services begins in earnest. The rubber meets the road as you focus like a laser beam on making **the best sale possible** so that when you leave the premises, you will do so with a signed order in your case and the prospect transitioning into becoming a customer. Please note that the 'best sale possible' does not always mean a sale with the biggest commission. It means a sale that makes the customer happy by its purchase. If, when you leave, the customer is not entirely happy with the purchase or with you, then s/he will often cancel the order before installation or delivery and the fat commission you mentally just put into your wallet will get pulled right back out again. I hate when that happens!

However, if you use consultative sales skills to guide the prospect through the sales process, then the **best sale possible** will often be the one that also **pays the highest commission.** And that happens when you take the time to ask the right questions to find out what would be best **for the prospect**, and that's what this chapter is all about. What needs, wants, and possibilities for the products and services you sell can you comfortably determine the prospect would like to have? For example, I *need* a car. I *want* a new car. I would love to have a brand new sportscar (possibility).

People in sales who don't use the consultative approach blow lots of sales they could have made. For example, not long ago my wife and I went out shopping for a new car. We drove onto the lot of a car dealer that sold the make of cars we were seriously considering, and to any salesman there, we were ideal prospects: middle-aged, arrived in an older but very high-end car, dressed well so most likely had money in the bank and excellent credit…perfect prospects. Had we encountered a salesperson who used consultative sales skills, we most likely would have driven away in a new car that day. But the salesman who approached us was fast-talking and pushy—essentially the very image of what most people expect to meet when they open their door to a door-to-door salesman!

The first words he said to us after he introduced himself was, *I'm gonna sell you a car today.* And he repeated that promise many times during our interaction. I guess he felt that was some kind of Jedi mind trick to plant the seed or something, but it didn't work. We even took a test drive with him in a car we liked, but his constant blather about how *he was gonna sell us a car today* pushed us into thinking and, as we left, saying, *No you're not.*

And he didn't. We drove off the lot in our car and went to a different dealer. The fact is that we would have bought a car from him had he asked us questions to discover what we liked in a car and then found one that fit what we wanted. A few simple questions like, *What do you want? What are you looking for? What do you like best in a new car?* But he didn't do any of that. He decided what he thought we should have (a top-of-the-line auto that no doubt paid a handsome commission) and pushed us into taking a test drive in that car. Mind you, we really liked the car he selected, and we bought one just like it later from a different dealer, but we didn't buy it from him because he was a crappy salesman who did not know or follow the consultative approach to sales. He pushed and we pushed back. He lost.

Question

There are only two types of questions that can be asked: open-ended and closed-ended. They can be used in many different ways with different titles like "confirming" or "closing," but the only two types of questions that exist, at their core, are **open** and **closed**. Knowing the difference between the two and being able to use them both comfortably and conversationally are critical success factors to being a good sales communicator who earns a very good living.

An open-ended question invites people to talk because open questions cannot be answered with one word. They are the opposite of a yes or no question. They do not begin with a verb and, instead, generally begin with words like *why, how, what,* or a short phrase like *please tell me*. They **invite people to talk**. When you ask someone an open-ended question, you invite them to expound about whatever it is you asked. An example of a good open question a cable TV rep would ask in the prospect's home to begin the discovery process would be...*Please tell me what you have now regarding high-speed internet, telephone service, and digital video (*try to include a mention of everything you can sell*)?* A person could, technically, answer that question with just one word—No. But if they felt that way then the rep would not have gotten past the door.

A closed-ended question, on the other hand, does not invite people to talk because it is a question that can be answered with just one word. A yes/no question is a perfect example of a closed-ended question. Do you have a computer? That's a closed question. Yes or no. I do, or I don't have a computer. Do you have a mobile phone? Do you come from another state? Do you watch movies? Do five closed questions in a row annoy you? These are all closed-ended, yes or no questions.

Poorly trained and undisciplined salespeople rely on closed questions to uncover needs. For cable TV reps, these tend to be *Do you have a television?* (Hey – some people don't.) *Do you have a computer? Do you have high-speed Internet? How fast is it? How much do you pay? Do you use a landline phone? Do you use cell phones?* Yak, yak, yak, yak. Here is a news bulletin: Asking three or more closed questions in a row is annoying. And asking direct questions about how much people pay can be—not to everyone, but to many (like me)—can be viewed as nosy. And annoying your prospects with repetitive closed and intrusive questions is not a good sales technique. That's why I refer to people who rely on just closed questions as badgers. Yak, yak, yak, yak, yak.

There are three simple reasons you should never ask a prospect how much they pay for anything they currently have. First, some people (like me) find a stranger asking questions about my payments for anything to be none of their business. Second, many prospects don't know because they don't pay that bill so they'll guess, and their guess will invariably be low, which puts your **super deal** at a disadvantage. And third, people lie. Yep, it is a sad fact that some prospects will knowingly lie and offer a low number to, again, make your super deal appear to be not so super.

The prospect will let you know how your deal stacks up against their current situation when the time is right, so why ask for trouble?

Listen

An open question will get the prospect to speak and while they speak, you **Listen** to what they say. Really pay attention and listen like your life depends upon it because your income certainly does. While they speak, you listen to hear the overlaps of why someone would want to own what you sell with what the prospect is saying they would like to have. Every overlap indicates a possible **need** or **want** they have that can be fulfilled by the features linked to the benefits of what you sell. So clearly each one you hear is a potential buy sign, and you need to exercise active listening to ferret them out into the open. But, if instead of actively listening you are simply waiting to talk, to wow them with your knowledge about your services, then you will not only miss important buy signs, but you will also piss off the prospect because they will know you are not paying attention to them. People like to be heard, and everyone can tell when the person with whom they are interacting is not listening.

Acknowledge

The dictionary tells us that acknowledge is a verb that means to "accept or admit the truth of."

In a sales conversation, **to acknowledge** means to let the prospect know that you are actively listening to what they say. Every time you hear a need, no matter how casually, you need to acknowledge the fact that you heard it. People like to be heard. Everyone does. And when you acknowledge what people say during a conversation it tells them you are listening and that they are being heard. This is huge. People like people who listen to them, and a prospect who likes you is much more likely to buy from you.

Being liked is important, but acknowledging every need heard also brings with it the profound benefit of the prospect seeing all on their own that **what they have may not be so good after all,** which opens the door to them seeing when you present to make the sale that what you have is what they really want. Bingo. The sale is set up and moving forward.

Q.L.A.Q. The Formula to Uncovering Buyer Needs

Q L A Q is how we use steps two, three, and four of the consultative sales process to comfortably and conversationally uncover buyer needs. It stands for Question - Listen - Acknowledge - Question. You start with step two, then step three, and step four before circling back to the beginning of the process at step two.

You need to use both open-ended and closed-ended questions for the **QLAQ** process to work. Start with a big **Open Question** (step 2) and while the prospect speaks, you **Listen** for needs (step 3). Every time you hear a potential need for your service (an overlap), you ask a simple **Closed Question** to **Acknowledge** the need you just heard (step 4). *Mr. Prospect, did I just hear you say… that your movies buffer a lot?…that you still have roaches after your current pest guy visited?* If you heard correctly the prospect will answer positively, and then you need to go right back to step two and ask another big **Open Question** to encourage the prospect to speak more while you **Listen** for more needs…which you also **Acknowledge** with a closed question, and then ask another **Open** question and on and on until you have uncovered as many needs as possible for what you sell. Question – Listen – Acknowledge – Question (again)

Closed questions are also a good way to steer the conversation. Let's say you are a cable TV rep, and your big open question was about Media Services and the prospect went on at length about just his Internet connection. You heard and acknowledged a couple of good needs, and the prospect did not go on to speak about any of his other services (TV, phone, home security, etc.). You want to uncover needs for everything you sell, so it's time to ask a closed question to get the conversation going in another direction. Like many MSOs today you may also offer a home security service package, so ask a closed question to go in that direction. *Are you ever concerned about security in this neighborhood?* After they respond go right into QLAQ and ask a big open question about home security.

Do not stop this **QLAQ** process until you have identified as many needs as possible for what you sell. The more needs **identified by you and acknowledged by the prospect** the easier it will be to make the sale (duh). It is a simple process that works but does require some practice at using both open and closed-ended questions in a comfortable and conversational manner. So practice. This is your life we're talking about, and if you want to have more money to boost your lifestyle, then practice these advanced sales skills until they come naturally.

Trap Warning

Be aware of a common trap many sales reps fall into when they successfully acknowledge a need heard. Instead of continuing with the QLAQ process to uncover **more** needs, they get excited that they've heard **a** need, and they launch right away into trying to make the sale. **Do not do this** because that one need may not be nearly enough to get the prospect to want to buy what you are selling. Follow the QLAQ process until **at least two needs** for everything you sell are identified. And by all means, do not forget that if you can't uncover any needs for one of the services you sell, then do not try to sell that specific service when you present because you will lose all credibility.

For highly competitive services, prospects need a reason to switch providers. By using the QLAQ process to uncover buyer needs, you will be satisfying the needs and wants the prospect has that are **not adequately met by their current provider,** which is all the reason they need to make the switch and buy from you.

5

How to Present and Close

Step up and make the sale...

Everything about the door-to-door sales process has led up to this point. You learned the mechanics of field activity, how to start the conversation at the door, and you comfortably and conversationally identified needs the prospect has for what you sell using the QLAQ process. In short, you are good-to-go, and it is time to make the sale and put some money in your pocket.

At the beginning of the last chapter on uncovering buyer needs, I warned about falling for the trap of The Salesman Dance. I start this chapter also with a few warnings about things to avoid so that you don't shoot yourself in the foot and blow the sale.

Three Deal Killers: The Three Don'ts

DK #1: DON'T start your sales presentation with the price of what you think they'll want to buy, because if you begin your presentation by throwing out a price, then you remind the prospect that speaking with you comes at a cost. Much like offering a handout with a price on it at the door gives some prospects a reason to say no and turn you away, leading with a dollar amount—regardless of the amount—when you present can be a negative attention grabber that turns some people off. Does it turn everyone off? Of course not. But if it gives just one prospect a reason to say no and turn you away, then that is one lost sale too many. Don't do it.

DK #2: DON'T keep selling after you've made the sale. Quit offering features and benefits after the prospect says, *I'll take it!*

I was field coaching a veteran sales rep one time, and he was doing well. At a house where we got past the door and inside the home, the man who invited us inside guided us both to sit on his living room couch. He volunteered, as we sat, that he and his wife had satellite service and that his wife would be home soon, and he needed her to be part of the conversation about possibly switching from satellite to our hardline service. Fine. While we waited for his wife, the sales rep used the QLAQ process to comfortably guide the conversation and uncover many needs for his triple play service bundle. The man's wife arrived, and she (naturally) asked her husband who we were. He told her we were with the local cable company, and before the rep and I had a chance to even get up off the couch and introduce ourselves, the woman asked if our company carried a certain channel. The rep I was with said *yes* and she immediately said *Great! We'll take it. Sign us up!* That was a pretty clear buy sign (duh) but, instead of pulling out an order form, the rep kept offering features and benefits about the video service she just told us she wanted to buy. He was a veteran sales rep so I did not step in, but I did give him a hard stare and indicated with my head that he should begin filling out the paperwork. He ignored my look and kept right on going with the features and benefits to the point where the woman and her husband gave each other a look that said to me they were tired of hearing the rep and were about to usher us out of their home. He was talking himself out of the sale, so I kicked him. Literally. I kicked him in his calf and said loud enough for both prospects to hear, *Good stuff. Brad will set up your installation.*

DK #3: DON'T offer any service for which no needs have been identified. Another time when I was field coaching a new-hire sales rep, we got inside a house and the rep started a good sales conversation with the prospect. During the conversation, the rep identified a number of needs for two of the services he sold but not the third. In fact, the prospect clearly stated that he did not want the third service. Sadly, the new hire did not listen to the prospect and presented for sale a bundle of his three services. And what's more, he kept offering the bundle until the prospect finally shut him off and showed us out with, *I'll tell you what guys,*

I've got to think about it. I've got your phone number. I'll give you a call. We left after blowing a sure double-play sale.

Think of a sales conversation as water flowing downhill. Your job throughout the entire sales process is to guide the conversation in a consistently positive manner by making comments and asking questions that are simply easier for the prospect to respond positively than negatively. Not impossible to say no, just easier to say yes. The easier you make it for the prospect to say yes, the more likely they are to do so. But every time you violate a *don't* you place an obstacle in the way of this smooth flowing conversational process. When flowing water meets an obstacle, it takes a different path. And when a sales conversation meets an obstacle, it may also take a path that leads you right out the door without a sale. Ouch. With sales, follow the '70s cool people mantra of *go with the flow*.

Okay. The stars are aligned, and you have uncovered buyer needs and want to present to your prospect the stuff you believe s/he will want to buy. But timing is important, so even though you think you have a slam dunk sale and a nice commission ready to land in your bank account, it is important to show patience. That's right. Don't rush.

As an example, I was field coaching a guy who was new to the job. We were working his leads, and we paused on the sidewalk in front of a house he had just knocked but got no answer. While marking that info on his leads, the people who lived in that house pulled into their driveway right next to where we were standing.

The rep greeted the young couple as they got out of their car, and he offered a nice opening to start a conversation. The first words the man said after he heard we were from the local cable company were, *We have satellite and hate it!* The new hire heard that and was just about to launch into his offers for digital video before I stepped in and said to the man, *We can help you with that, but first please tell us about all of your media services. Where's a good place for us to sit down?*

Video looked like a slam dunk sale, but before the rep started selling, I wanted to get in the house and see why the prospect hated his satellite service to make sure the video sale would, in fact, be a slam dunk. I also wanted to see if needs existed for other media services. After all, the prospect didn't say *We hate satellite and want to buy everything you've got.* He just said *We have satellite and hate it!* I wanted the rep to help the couple as much as possible, while earning a bigger commission with a bigger sale. So I went into the QLAQ process to uncover as many needs as possible to see how much the prospect might buy. It turned out to be a big sale, and the couple got great value and the sales rep earned a much bigger commission than if he had just settled on a video-only sale.

Patience pays off. Try it!

Pre-Close

You are ready to present and close the sale, and you feel the prospect is ready to buy. Good stuff. Everything is going along swimmingly. However, I don't want to rain on anyone's parade, but sometimes the prospect will say no to your close even when you do everything by the (my) book. At the end of even the best sales conversation, where you and the prospect are both smiling and nodding your heads, the prospect may still object to the sale and say no when you ask for the sale. It sucks, but it happens. I will show you how to overcome objections in the next chapter, but since the easiest objection to overcome is the one you never get, asking a pre-close question **before you present** is an excellent way to avoid any deal-killing objections at the end when you try to close the sale.

A pre-close question is simply a soft and friendly way to ask for any objections upfront so that you can be proactive and maintain control of the sales conversation. A pre-close will let you **test the waters** so to speak to see if the customer is ready to move forward. Think of it as a batter's warmup swing as s/he steps up to the plate.

If the response to your pre-close is positive, then continue with your presentation and close the sale. But if you do get an objection, it's like you get a **do-over** to avoid a no later on. This do-over gives you the chance to uncover more needs or address an obstacle you were unaware of that could blow the sale. Their response to your pre-close will let you know if the sales conversation has been going along as swimmingly as you feel it has.

Here are a few examples of good pre-close questions. Pick the one best for the sales situation you are in and use it.

- *All things being equal, is there anything that we have missed in our discussion that would keep you from buying my product?*
- *I am not promising that I can, but If I can make this fit your monthly budget, would there be anything that we have not discussed that would keep you from adding X service today?* (The "If I could, would you?" type of close)
- *Mr./Mrs. Customer, you shared with me your concerns about the reliability of your existing service, and we discussed how my service addresses the reliability concern. Is there anything that I am not aware of that would prevent you from moving forward with an installation of my service?*
- *Mr./Mrs. Customer, if I can show you how you will get a much better value with my service, will there be any reason to not move forward with an agreement today?*

Get past the pre-close and step up the plate to hit a home run and put money in your pocket.

The Formula to Present:
How to Make the Sale

Think of my **Formula to Present** as a recipe and, like any recipe that results in a tasty dish, every part must be used for the result to be right. You would not think of leaving out an ingredient of the recipe to bake a cake and expect the cake to turn out well, would you? Of course not. So don't expect the presentation to work out well and lead to a closed sale if you leave part of it out either. Every one of these components must be included when you present for the recipe to work, for the cake to turn our right. For you to be successful.

Here is the simple formula to comfortably guide prospects into seeing that what you sell is what they want to buy: **E + F + B + CQ**. It stands for **Enthusiasm – Features – Benefits – Confirming Question.** Done right, a positive response to the confirming question leads directly to a successful close. See? Piece of cake (pun intended).

Here's an example of what it looks like in real life: *I've got great news for you! My formula to present will show you how to make more sales and put more money in your pocket. How does that sound?*

Let me break down the example above into the specific steps of the formula:

Start with **E. Enthusiasm** is contagious. Set the stage for a good reception with an Enthusiastic statement about what's to come and the prospect will naturally expect to hear something they will like. Remember the adage; "if you believe it, others will too." Simple as that.

- *I've got great news for you...* (Prospect can't help but think, *What?*)

Follow with **F**. Offer a **Feature** which is the specific product or service you want the prospect to buy.

- *My formula to present...* (In this case, I want you to believe me and mentally buy my Formula to Present.)

Now come in with the **B**. People buy benefits so give the prospect something to buy. Link the feature you want the prospect to buy to the **Benefit** the prospect will gain with its purchase.

- *...will show you how to make more sales and put more money in your pocket.* (That's a clear benefit to using the formula, right?)

End presentation with **CQ;** Which is a closed-ended, yes/no **Confirming Question.** This is **not a closing question** because I am not asking you to buy anything. Not yet. I am simply asking if you like **what I just said**. And since what I just said satisfies needs identified, then it is easier to answer with a yes than a no. Like water flowing downhill...

- *How does that sound?*

The Importance of Using Confirming Questions

Confirming questions are a critical component of the consultative sales process because they let you know how smoothly the water of the sales conversation is flowing. *How's that sound? Does that sound like a good value to you? Does that sound like something your renters would appreciate?* Any of these are good closed-ended confirming questions and how the prospect responds will let you know how you are doing. For example, during the QLAQ discovery process, you use them to see if you heard the prospect correctly whenever s/he mentions a possible need. *Mr. Prospect, did I just hear you say...?* And you use them in the **E-F-B-CQ Formula to Present** as regular confirmation that your presentation is on the right track.

Every time the prospect agrees with your confirming question during your presentation s/he is saying *yes, that's right*, which sets you up for a successful close because all the yesses build up to where the actual closing question of *Will you buy my stuff?* becomes just another yes and, bingo, the sale is made. Piece of cake.

Let me remind you that no one is a born salesman. Being gregarious is often mistaken for sales skills, but I have personally met boring people who make a lot of money at sales because they learned the process and practiced it until it became second nature. So practice asking confirming questions. Practice all the time, practice with your friends, your family, your spouse, your kids, your neighbors, everyone. *How's that sound? Would that work for you? Are you with me?* All of those are simple yes/no confirming questions. Practice, practice, practice.

Issues Regarding Closing the Sale

You collected a pocket full of yeses from your presentation so now it's time to ask for their business to close the sale. But first, let me share a couple of points regarding the common fear among salespeople of actually asking for the business and closing the sale.

The first is to point out that you have gone through a fairly lengthy sales conversation with the prospect, especially if it's a **competitive switch** sale. You had a long conversation with the prospect. You established a rapport, and you got along with that person. You are both being friendly to each other. Often the fear erupts when it comes to actually ask for the sale because you don't want to spoil the wonderful sense of camaraderie created over the course of the sales conversation. Okay, but to that I say RUBBISH! The whole camaraderie is based upon the sales process. You have been in a sales conversation so you will spoil nothing by asking for the sale. The prospect expects it. Making a sale is why you are there! Don't wait for them to sell themselves. You have no business unless you ask for the business. So get over that. You can still be friends afterwards but follow through after you present and complete the reason you met in the first place—to make a sale—so ask for the business and close the sale.

The second point I want to make is that when people say they have a hard time closing, it is not that they are afraid to ask, it is that they keep hearing no when they do ask because they failed in their job up to that point. They did not do the work of building a good sale. They did not uncover needs accurately so they presented poorly, and when they tried to close, they asked a closing question that was easier to answer with a no than a yes. So they got the no. They put obstacles in the way of the water flowing downhill so it got sidetracked, and instead of flowing into a green pool of money that earned a commission, it acted as a slip and slide and shot them out the door. Bye-bye. Better luck next time!

Three Types of Closes: Ask for the Business!

First and foremost is what I call the **Universal Close,** and it's called that because it is universal. *If I can, will you?* Is an extremely powerful verbal tool in the sales process and is used by salespeople everywhere to close sales.

You established a good rapport, uncovered multiple needs, and asked the prospect a pre-close question before you presented. The process was going well so you presented and during your presentation, the prospect agreed multiple times that what you said made good sense. S/he liked what you said. So here is a simple yet accurate example of how to use the **Universal Close** to ask for the sale:

Good stuff, Mr. Prospect. We've identified a number of areas where my bundled package of services will make your life easier. ***If I can*** *get everything to you at a price you can afford,* ***will you*** *buy it all?*

*...****If I can*** *package everything for you into 10 easy-to-handle monthly payments,* ***will you*** *sign right now?*

See? Piece of cake.

The next type of closing question is the **Assumed Close**. It is probably the most common close used in sales of video, internet, and telephone service because, by the time you get to this point to ask for the business, they've said yes so many times that why on Earth wouldn't they want it? So you just *assume* they do want it, and you ask for the sale...*Ok, will next Wednesday be a good time to get your service installed?* Just assume they're going to want it. Period. Assume it. If you have done your job up to that point, then that is exactly what will happen. *Hey man, this is going great. OK then! What do you say we fix you up with an install time for the day after tomorrow? Or ... I'll call in and get the best time I can for you, ok? Great.*

The third type of close is the **Direct Close**. Generally, the time for this type of close is after you tried a different close and, although you didn't hear no, you also didn't hear yes. The prospects are vacillating and simply can't make the decision to buy. They've come up to the hurdle and they just can't step over it. So you need to give them just a little push. A nudge in the right direction. So here is what I've done many times selling bundled packages for cable operators that has worked very well:

The couple I've been with are at that point and the man and the woman are looking at each other back and forth, and one of them is kind of rubbing his hands. You can tell that they are close to saying yes. They want it, but they simply cannot make the decision to buy. They just can't step over that hurdle. In these situations I say to them, *Hey you're not buying a car. Come on, it's cable media services. That's all, give it a shot. Ok? Let's go.* Or... *You're not buying a car or a new house for goodness' sake, it's entertainment and convenience. Let's go.* I say these things in a lighthearted and upbeat tone of voice, and just about every time the tension evaporates and one or both of the prospects smile and say, *OK. Let's do it!* Ka-Boom! Money in the bank.

These three types of closes are very simple and very common. Be aware of the fact that during your sales conversation your entire conversation and all the wonderful friendly camaraderie you established with the prospect is **based upon making a sale.** So follow through and **ask for the business**.

If your close ratio is very poor, then you are not laying the proper foundation of uncovering needs and presenting to satisfy needs identified with the features linked to the benefits of your product. Go back and practice the previous steps that lead to the close.

Analyze & Review

I urge you to use immediate analysis of every sales encounter. Every time you go through the process and you make a sale, analyze and focus on what went well. Congratulate yourself but do not fail to notice the parts that could have been better. Were you a bit too pushy at one point? If so, how did you rescue the conversation? And of course, those times when it doesn't work, think about and analyze to see where and when everything went off the rails. How did I blow that sale? Did I talk too much? Did I not talk enough? Did I actively listen or just wait to talk?

Visualize and be your own sales coach. Evaluate every single sales conversation—good, bad, or ugly. By doing this you can go back to that skill set in need of improvement and work on it, practice it, and master it. By sticking to this process and strengthening each skill to the point of mastery, you will become a master of sales and make your dreams come true.

Important Takeaways

I will wrap up these last couple of chapters with a few takeaways. First, uncover As Many Needs As Possible before you present—AMNAP. Otherwise, you are just asking someone *Hey do you want to buy what I've got?* And that's a question that's pretty darn easy to answer with a no than a yes.

Next, begin and maintain good enthusiasm throughout the entire sales conversation. I do not mean you should go cheerleader, just focus on always being upbeat and positive. Positive energy is contagious. *If you believe it, others will too.* Prospects will feel the positive energy and just about everyone likes to be around positive people.

Next, when you offer a bundled package of services, present one item at a time. *Hey, we've got this great package of stuff you are going to love!* And then present each package component one piece at a time using the E-F-B-CQ Formula to Present. If you gain agreement on every individual component, then buying the big package is just another yes.

And last but by no means least, always ask for the sale. Always, always close. In those rare instances when you do everything right but when you ask for the business they still say **no**, that's called an objection, and that's what I'll handle in the next chapter.

6

Overcoming Objections

When does the act of selling begin?

A few decades ago the manager of a sales team I was on posed the question, "When does the act of selling begin?" during a sales meeting. None of us got it right and a few responses were just downright dumb. One of the guys on the team who used to sell insurance, I think, said, *Well, selling begins when I put my pants on in the morning...* Another said, *When I stick my hand out.* But my favorite was the guy who said, *When I look them in the eye!* (Really? Was he trying to stare the prospect into making a purchase?)

I didn't get it right either, which is why I pose the same question in every workshop I conduct. When does the act of selling begin? Good question and I'll answer it with a story about a brake job.

I used to drive a 1994 Lincoln Town Car. Big, heavy, comfortable. I loved that car and kept it running for many years by always paying attention to regular maintenance. Every 3000 miles I changed the oil. Without fail. Whenever the odometer logged another 3000 miles, I changed the oil. I frequented the same place a few times because of their coupons (Everybody likes a deal!) and every time I arrived the clerk took my coupon and my car keys and had a mechanic drive my car into a service bay. A glass wall separated their lounge from the service bays so I could watch the mechanic change the oil. When he finished, I paid the bill, exchanged smiles with the clerk, and drove away, good for another 3000 miles.

But one time something different occurred. Everything was the same until the mechanic raised my car on a lift and began draining the oil. While it drained, he came to me in the waiting room and asked me a question, *Mr. Robinson. How about I check your brakes while your car is up on the rack?* Ok, he's a mechanic, and my car was stopping just fine, but I believed in regular maintenance, and I was there already, so I told him to go ahead. I watched as he pulled off a wheel and examined the brake pads. He then brought the pads to me in the waiting room to show me how badly they were worn. I knew what bad brake pads looked like, and he was telling the truth. My brakes were almost completely shot. When brakes go out while you're driving, bad things can happen. In addition to possible personal injury, once your wheels go steel on steel the cost of repair is significantly higher than just replacing the pads when they are worn.

I agreed the pads were bad, and he asked me another question. *How about I fix the brakes while you're here and your car is already up on the lift?* He was right that I needed new brakes, and it was convenient for me to have them done right away, so I said ok...And I bought a brake job from him.

When I tell this story in my workshops, I ask everyone if he a salesman. After all, he asked me to make a purchase, and I did. I bought a brake job from him. I spent a couple of hundred dollars instead of just $25...So, was he a salesman?

Most people in the room say yes, of course, he is a salesman because he sold me a brake job. But the correct answer is no. Not at all. He was a mechanic from the start of the oil change to the finish of the brake job because every time he asked me a question, I said yes. He asked to check my brakes, and I said *Yes.* He asked for the business to fix the brakes, and I again said, *Yes. Go ahead.*

If I had said no when he asked to repair my brakes, then he would have then been faced with the choice of remaining a mechanic and walking away, which many of them do, or to become a salesman and try to find out why I said no to the brake job that we both knew I needed.

So the correct answer to my sales manager's long-ago question, *when does the act of selling begin? Is **when you hear the first no.*** If you never hear no, then you are providing customer service, which is a good thing. The mechanic provided me with excellent customer service by helping me identify a need I didn't know I had, and then he helped me satisfy that need in the most convenient (I was already at the shop.) and economical (cheaper to replace pads than to repair damaged wheels) manner possible. Truly excellent customer service.

You are a door-to-door salesperson and hearing no is an expected part of the sales process. So when you hear no, it is time to put your game face on and go to work to find out why the prospect said no and then overcome that no to keep the sale moving forward.

If I had objected by saying no to either of the mechanic's questions, he would have been faced with the decision to remain a mechanic and walk away, which some mechanics would do because, let's face it, they're mechanics, or become a salesman and try to overcome my objection by finding out why I said no.

I point this out because we as salespeople are faced with objections from start to finish of every encounter and it is absolutely critical that we know how to overcome them smoothly and comfortably so that we can keep the sale moving forward.

Mastering the formula to overcome any objection takes attention and practice. This means buckle up because I present a lot of specific how-to content in the following three major components of this chapter.

In the first component, I point out **five facts about overcoming objections**. In the next, I clarify the **four types or categories of objections** that exist. There are only four, and I call them the 4 Ds. And in the third component, I share with you **the three to**

four-step proven process to overcome almost any objection.

Five Facts About Overcoming Objections

#1: Selling Begins at the First No

Selling begins at the first objection. The first objection usually comes right at the door, and you have to get past it to keep the sale moving forward. When you hear an objection to your opening, try at least three times to get past it using the rebuttal formula: **Overcoming Common Objections at the Door** that I gave you at the end of Chapter Two. If you still can't sell the sales conversation to the prospect, then start to walk away and use the Name/Number technique to capture their name and phone number for a follow-up call where you will hopefully find them in a better mood.

#2: Arguing Never Works

Good grief, I hear that all the time when I coach reps. People object to their pitch and respond negatively with something like, *No I don't want your product. Your company stinks*, or *you are too expensive,* and the rep comes back with...*no it doesn't*. Uh, yes it does. Your company stinks. *No, it doesn't*...It's too much money...*No, it isn't*. Arguing does not work. Period. But that's what most people do when they think they are overcoming objections. But the fact is they are simply arguing instead of following the set, and proven, process to overcome objections that I present here in my book. I sincerely hope you'll be able to focus at the end of this chapter on the times that you heard no and how you acted to see if you were arguing instead of trying to clarify and overcome the objection. Arguing does not work.

#3: Objections Can Come at Any Time

We hear them a lot right at the Opening At The Door...right? And we often hear them throughout the entire sales process...pretty much every time you hear the word but, an objection follows. That word is like the bell ringer. When you are in a sales conversation and the prospect says...*Yeah, but...* be ready because the next thing he says will be an objection you must overcome to keep moving the sale forward.

#4: You Must Understand and Isolate an Objection in Order to Overcome it

You see, here's where people argue, because when somebody says *no...no thanks...* instead of trying to understand why the prospect is saying no, they just start throwing out information. *No? Well, how about this, and how about that, and the other thing and blah, blah, blah, blah...* You have no idea if you are hitting the target because you don't know what the target is. You don't know why they are saying no. For illustration purposes, I want you to think of an objection as your opponent in a boxing match. You are both in the ring and you want to win the fight. You want to make that sale by hitting your opponent—the objection—with a knock-out punch. Right? BAM! Objection overcome. Sale moving forward. But if you do not first find out the reason behind their objection then it is like you are in the ring with your eyes closed. And it doesn't take a genius to know that if you can't see your opponent, then you're not going to hit him very many times. *Oh, he's got his eyes closed. Here watch this!* And your opponent – the objection – wins and your sale is knocked out. You lose. You need to see your target. You need to understand what it is they are objecting to for you to have any hope of winning the fight and keeping the sale moving forward.

#5: When You Ask What They're Objecting to, the First Thing They Say is Overwhelmingly the Real Reason

People will give you a whole string of reasons as to why they're saying no. So you need to really listen. I have mentioned a hundred times the need to truly listen and not just wait to talk. You need to listen to their reasons so that you hear the first thing they say because that is the objection you need to overcome.

When someone objects and says no at the end of the sale, after you have uncovered needs and used the formula to present and then asked for the business: *Ok then, let's schedule your installation* ... but the prospect comes back with a *Nah, nah... I don't think so.* Then you need to understand why they are saying no, so you ask them...*Why not?* And the person says...***Well, I need to talk it over with my wife***, *but at the same time it's a lot of money, the hassle of getting it installed, I don't know about your customer service...yadda, yadda, yadda, yadda...* all of this other stuff is fluff. The real reason is that he needs to bring his wife into the equation. Period. It happens. Keep in mind that you are winning back customers from the competition, and your products and services have a lot of moving parts! Cable TV services used to be a one-call close sale. But in today's high-tech world of so many moving parts—not to mention the higher monthly bill—a good rep has to be accustomed to multi-call closes.

The Four Types of Objections: The Four Ds

Only four types or categories of objections exist, and I call them the four Ds. Every objection you will hear in your life falls into one of these four categories.

The first D is DRAWBACK. A drawback is something negative that gives the prospect a clear reason to not move forward. The most common drawback to the sale of anything is price, but it could be a host of other types of issues as well, like installation, service issues, or simply negative past experiences with your company's customer service.

The Second D is DOUBT. In short, they don't believe you! That's right, they do not believe what you are telling them. They doubt the price you quote will remain the same as long as you tell them it will but, instead, think the price will jump 500% after just a couple of months. They don't believe that the installer/service person will be there on time. They do not believe that customer service has improved since the last time they were a customer but quit to go to your competitor. They don't believe you.

The 3rd D is they DON'T CARE. They are indifferent. Indifference is the toughest type of objection to overcome because when they don't care, it means that you did not follow the consultative sales process as outlined in this book before you asked for the sale. You must follow the proven process step-by-step every time...uncover as many needs as possible...then present with enthusiasm, offering features linked to benefits that satisfy needs identified, followed by a confirming question. You must do all of this **before** you try to close the sale. If you skip any step, then you are not doing your job and you hear things like...*Nahhh, I like what I have. No. Never mind. I need to think about it. I'll call you later, bye.* And you're done.

The 4th D is they DON'T GET IT. They misunderstand. They misunderstood an important part of your presentation, so they see a drawback where none exists, and they say no. Maybe you weren't clear when you discussed the pricing structure, the service dates, or you mumbled when you offered a two-hour installation window so they believe they will have to wait around all day to get installed and that won't work for them, so they say no. People instinctively say no when they are confused.

Properly identifying the type of objection you hear is critical because each type has its own very specific offset to overcome it.

Here are each of the four Ds with their specific offset:

- Offset a **Drawback** with **benefits**
- **Offset Doubt** with **proof**
- **Offset Don't Care** with **questions** to uncover needs not previously identified
- **Offset Don't Get It** with **clarity**

I covered five important facts about overcoming objections and identified the four types of objections you'll ever hear. Now I'll give you the four-step process to overcome an objection—regardless its type.

The Four-Step Process to Overcome any Objection

1) **Understand**
    a. You need to understand why they are saying no.

2) **Acknowledge**

    a. You need to let them know that you hear their objection.

3) **Respond**

    a. You need to respond to their objection with the proper offset *according to its type.*

4) **Validate**

    a. You need to confirm your attempt to overcome their objection with a closed-ended question.

Step #1: Understand

If the prospect volunteers their reason for saying no, which mostly happens right at the door and not later in the sales process while you are trying to sell your services, then there is no need to clarify, and you skip right to step two and Acknowledge it. A *No* at the door is usually connected to the reason for it. *I had you before and you stink!*

But when they do not volunteer their reason, then you need to know why they are saying no so that you can properly identify its type (Which D is it?) and use the proper offset to overcome it and keep the sale moving forward. There are a lot of different ways of getting them to tell you, but my favorite is to simply ask, *Really, why?*

You have had a conversation with the person during which you established a rapport. You are getting along, so when you get an objection, it is not being pushy at all to simply ask *why?* in a comfortable tone of voice and demeanor. You want to know. I find that punctuating my query with physical actions helps a great deal at getting them to open up and tell me the reason they are objecting. This is what I have done countless times with much success...I scrunch my eyes a little bit and tilt my head to the side like a dog does when he's trying to understand, and I spread my arms open with my palms facing up and just ask, *Why?* Many times I do the same physical actions but just say, *Oh?* Which conveys the question without having to actually ask it, ***What do you mean? What the heck! Why aren't you buying this good stuff!*** People will open up. This move is simple, and it works.

Whether you ask outright or give them the head tilt of incredulity, *Oh?* they will give you an answer, and you need to listen like your life depends upon it because the first thing they say is the real objection. They may list a bunch of stuff but, as I said earlier, the first thing they offer is overwhelmingly the main reason for their objection—the main reason they are saying no. That is your target. That is your opponent in the ring. Once you clarify the objection and identify its type, you know which offset to use to overcome it.

Here is a good life news bulletin: Identifying each type of objection and memorizing the offsets for each type takes work. No one is a natural at this. This is advanced sales and being able to **quickly, accurately,** and **conversationally** overcome objections during the sales process is the separator between those salespeople doing okay and those who consistently earn big commission checks. Do your homework and practice.

Step #2: Acknowledge

To acknowledge what people say is an important part of good verbal communication because people like to be heard, and acknowledging what you hear tells the person with whom you are speaking that you are listening to what they say and not just waiting to talk.

Whenever you get an objection, an invisible and impenetrable wall comes down between you and the prospect. With an objection, suddenly the conversation changes from friendly to adversarial, and you switch from being a friendly representative of your company to a ruthless tool for the evil company trying to push them into buying something they don't want. Bummer. You need to get rid of that wall, or you're done, and the only way to do that is to acknowledge that the wall is there. Acknowledge its existence and it will go away.

You ask for the sale, and they say no and the wall comes down. Ka–Blam! You ask why, and they respond with, *Well, you don't carry my favorite sports channel, and I need to talk it over with my wife, consult my astrologer, talk with my gerbil, and my neighbor always has something to say, so I better speak with him too...*You paid attention and hear the main reason he said no is because you don't carry his favorite sports channel. Everything else he says is secondary (Well, maybe not the parts about the gerbil or the neighbor…). You now get rid of the wall by acknowledging what he said and, in the process, add to the positive impact of your acknowledgement with a little something extra to show how well you do understand. You say… *I can appreciate that. The channel you want is a good channel. I get that.* Vroom. Wall is gone and you are back to being buddies. And then, since the missing channel is a drawback, you offset the drawback with other benefits.

Always acknowledge an objection. If you don't acknowledge its existence, then it will stay in place, and you will soon be leaving without a sale.

Step #3: Respond

Almost in the same breath after you acknowledge the objection, you **respond** with the proper offset for that type of objection.

Now you see how critical it is that you are able to quickly and accurately identify the type of objection voiced…whatever it is. Which D did the prospect voice to derail the sale? Was it a drawback, a doubt, that he doesn't care or that he doesn't get it? It takes practice to be able to quickly and accurately identify an objection's type, but you've got to be able to do it because each type of objection has its own very specific offset. And you will fail in your attempt to get your sale back on track if you use the wrong offset in your response.

You **understand** the objection and identify its type. Then you **acknowledge** the objection and **respond** with its proper offset.

Step #4: Validate

Here's where you pull it all together to keep the sale moving forward. You understand what they're objecting to. You acknowledge their objection. You respond according to its type, and then you ask the prospect a yes/no **Confirming Question** to see what s/he thinks of your attempt to overcome the objection.

How's that sound? Doesn't that sound like a good value? These are not closing questions because you are not asking them to commit to a purchase. This process to overcome an objection sets up for your next attempt to close the sale because if the prospect agrees with your confirming question, then ask again for the sale. Simple as that. Keep doing this until the prospect runs out of objections and decides to buy what you're selling.

Step #5: Close Again!

Okay. I sneaked this one in, but you should have seen it coming because what do you do after the prospect agrees with your confirming question? You again ask for the sale! Duh.

Examples of How it's Done

Each of the following four examples starts with the prospect objecting after the sales rep tries to close the sale. See how the objection is Clarified and then overcome using the U.A.R.V. four-step process.

Example #1: A Drawback is offset with Benefits

Rep: *Okay then. How about I get your service installed next Tuesday?*

Prospect: *No. Not yet. I'm not ready to switch.*

Rep with **Step #1**: *Why not?*

Prospect: *Well, **you don't carry my favorite sports channel**, and I need to talk it over with my wife. And I can't afford to wait around all day for the installer.*

Rep with **Steps 2–4**: Acknowledge/Respond/Validate

*I understand. **That is a good channel. But you did say** the four other sports channels we carry are also good channels, and that you will save money every month with my service compared to what you're paying now. So doesn't replacing one sports channel with four new sports channels and getting a better value every month **sound like a good idea?***

Prospect: *Yeah. That does sound good.*

Rep with **2nd close attempt** (sneaky Step #5): *All right then. Let's schedule that install. Okay?*

Prospect: *Sure. Let's do it.*

Example #2: Doubt is offset with Proof

Rep: *Okay then. How about I get your service installed next Tuesday?*

Prospect: *No. Not yet. I'm not ready to switch.*

Rep with **Step #1**: Oh? *Why not?*

Prospect: *Well, I like everything you said, but **I know the price will go up every month** right after I get installed. And I need to talk it over with my wife.*

Rep with **Steps 2-4**: Acknowledge/Respond/Validate

I get that. *No one wants to pay more for something than they were told it would cost. Really. I get that. **So I will put in writing that the price will not go up a full year.***

How does that sound?

Prospect: *That sounds pretty good.*

Rep with **2nd close attempt** (sneaky Step #5): *Okay then. Let's get you hooked up.*

Prospect: *Okay. Let's do it.*

Example #3: Don't Care is offset with Questions

Rep: *Okay then. How about I get your installation scheduled for next Tuesday?*

Prospect: *No. I don't think so.*

Rep with **Step #1**: Oh?

Prospect: *I just don't want to switch right now. But I have your number and will call you when I'm ready.*

Rep with **Step #2** and a prayer that s/he can get the sale back on track: **I get that**. *There's a lot going on nowadays.*

Please tell me about your media services.

Prospect: *No. I have someplace to go right now. So, I'll call you later when I'm ready.*

Rep: *I understand. But if I can get you a better value every month, would you give me more time to discuss services?*

Prospect: *I don't have time. Goodbye.*

Rep: *But, but, but* (as you are ushered out the door. Next time do your job and ask questions to uncover needs **before** you ask for the sale!):

Example #4: Don't Get It is offset with Clarity

Rep: *Okay then. How about I get your service installed next Tuesday?*

Prospect: *Not yet. I'm not ready to switch.*

Rep with **Step #1**: Oh? *Why not?*

Prospect: **I can't afford to wait around all day for the installer**. *Plus, I'll bet the price will go up every month right after I get installed. And I need to talk it over with my wife…*

Rep with **Steps 2-4**: Acknowledge/Respond/ Validate

I get that. *No one wants to waste a day waiting for the installer to show up. But I must **not have been clear earlier**. Because the good news is that my company hired a lot of new installers, so we now offer **a two-hour window** for installation. Doesn't that sound doable?*

Prospect: *Yeah. I can do that.*

Rep with **2nd close attempt** (sneaky Step #5): *Okay then. Let's get you hooked up.*

Prospect: *Okay. Let's do it.*

It is important to focus and practice being able to quickly and accurately identify and categorize the objections you'll hear because one can be used a couple of different ways. For example, if the person says *no, I don't want it,* and you ask why and they say *I can't just wait around all day for the install. I just can't spare the time.* All right. On the surface that is a drawback because waiting around all day is a negative that you offset with benefits. **But you had already mentioned the availability of two-hour install window, so his objection morphed from a drawback into a misunderstanding which you offset with clarity**.

Now you clear up the misunderstanding and ask again for the sale and boom! Money in the bank.

This proven process to overcoming objections works but takes practice to get it right. So do that. Practice. Just like major league baseball players before each game...practice!

Buttoning Up the Sale

Hearing yes is not the end of the sale. There is critical work yet to do. Sometimes customers change their mind after you leave and cancel their install or service appointment—I hate it when that happens! But you can influence this action and many times prevent it because a canceled sale usually comes from a sloppy finish to the sales process. Your company wants another happy customer, and you want a sales commission, so everything in your power to button up the sale to ensure it gets fully completed. You need to **finalize** the sale by cleanly managing their expectations and reinforcing the decision they made to switch to your company.

Review the **features and benefits** of every product and service they ordered and remind them of the great value they will receive. It is helpful to use a guide for this step, and I like the idea of using whichever document you were using when they said yes.

Compliment them on their decision. If two people are there ask each of them what they are most looking forward to so they can hear each other's excitement. This also allows them to remind themselves why they are ordering. This reinforces their decision and gets them excited about the service. If they are excited, they are more likely to be home for the installation or service appointment. And who isn't excited by a service installer or, regarding pest control, an exterminator coming by. (okay... Maybe *excited* is the wrong word for anticipating the bug guy's upcoming visit.)

Ask for referrals for a couple of reasons. Of course, so that you can get some good sales leads. But also because if they give a friend or neighbor's name to you for a direct follow-up, then they are much more likely to be home for their install/service appointment. Let's face it, it would be pretty damn tacky for someone to refer a neighbor but not get installed themselves. So if someone gives you a referral, they will be more likely to get installed and to present you, the service, and your company in a positive light.

Referrals are a warm sale and getting good at asking for them can be the difference between a JOB—which stands for *just over broke* and achieving all of your goals. Let me state the obvious here—when you get referrals, follow up on them *immediately!*

Finally, leave behind materials with your pending customer that will keep selling the services after you leave the home. I would leave a channel lineup, sell sheet, and or comparison sheet. Always leave them your business card and reiterate they should call you—nobody else—with any questions.

Shake their hands before leaving and say *Thank you for your order and welcome to the* (name of your company) *family* (I know that sounds corny, but I've done it and it works well).

A Few Final (*Profound*) Thoughts

The late, great comedian John Belushi once did a skit on Saturday Night Live that starts with him speaking into a microphone at a big annual dinner celebration of some business benevolent association similar to the Lions Club and the like. His bit is to introduce the keynote speaker for the evening—a famous retired Hall of Fame professional baseball player (played by Garrett Morris) who Belushi and all members of his club had long admired. In his lengthy introduction, Belushi goes on and on about how thrilled he and the entire club are to have this famous baseball player speak at their dinner. He specifically mentions in his intro that it took their entire club treasury to make it happen. When his introduction finally came to an end, the retired ballplayer, who was originally from a Spanish-speaking Caribbean country, steps up to the mic to deliver his speech. Anticipation was thick and expectations were off the chart. He nodded his head to acknowledge a few people and delivered his speech. He said, *"Baseball has been berry good to me."* Then he sat down. Speech over. Treasury gone.

When I started in door-to-door sales, I would have killed to have someone who knew what the hell they were doing tell or show me how to do this job. Not just how to sell, I was already pretty good at that, but what, exactly, did I have to do to be **consistently successful selling door-to-door.** Training programs abound both then and now, but none on them—none of them—were created by and presented by someone who was a successful door-to-door sales rep who knocked on doors in both good weather and bad and in all types of neighborhoods and had the cops called on him a few times for being in that well-to-do building or high-end neighborhood until now.

This book is my story. I wrote it. It is a blueprint to success.

Since I started my door-to-door journey decades ago, I've gone from bankruptcy to having purchased four nice homes (not all at once - duh). I've put my two children through major universities. I created a company that generated millions of dollars in revenue and, frankly, life is good. I now write, I speak, and I do whatever I can to help other door-to-door sales reps succeed.

To (kind of) quote Garret Morris, "Door-to-door sales has been very, very good to me."

To you and to all who sell door-to-door, I wish you luck and good selling!

Printed in the United States
by Baker & Taylor Publisher Services